10
Steps to
Successful

Budgeting

Lianabel Oliver and
Eduardo Nin

atd
PRESS

21 20 19 18   1 2 3 4 5

ATD Press is an internationally renowned source of insightful and practical information on talent development, training, and professional development.

ATD Press
1640 King Street
Alexandria, VA 22314 USA

Ordering information: Books published by ATD Press can be purchased by visiting ATD's website at www.td.org/books or by calling 800.628.2783 or 703.683.8100.

Library of Congress Control Number: 2018962008

ISBN-10: 1-947308-86-6
ISBN-13: 978-1-947308-86-2
e-ISBN: 978-1-947308-87-9

ATD Press Editorial Staff
Director: Kristine Luecker
Manager: Melissa Jones
Community of Practice Manager, Management: Ryan Changcoco
Developmental Editor: Kathryn Stafford
Text and Cover Design: Darrin Raaum

Printed by Marquis, Montmagny, Quebec

CONTENTS

Preface

We started writing this book before Hurricanes Irma and María ravaged Puerto Rico, the island where we live and work. Before Hurricane Irma, we were preoccupied with the normal ups and downs of daily living. Although Irma caused major damage in some parts of the island, we were confident that power could be restored quickly and normalcy would return soon. Then, on September 20, God opened the floodgates of Hell. Still reeling from Irma, we were unprepared for the force and devastation that María brought to the island. There was a Puerto Rico "before María," and now there is a Puerto Rico "after María." Our lives have changed forever.

Despite the hurricanes, we continued writing this book, albeit under suboptimal conditions—no water, no power, no Internet access, no cable TV. Because this book is about planning and budgeting, we can tell you that no amount of planning can prepare you for what statisticians called a "black swan event," a term coined by Nassim Nicholas Taleb, a finance professor, writer, and former Wall Street trader. *Black swans* are high impact events, which are unexpected and unpredictable. Hurricane María was our black swan.

Although you cannot plan for a black swan event, you can certainly prepare for one, particularly in the case of natural disasters. There is a lot of value to planning, which is the underlying foundation of a budget, both on a personal and professional level. Planning can help you assess the external factors that may represent opportunities or threats to your business. It can also help you examine your strengths and weaknesses as an organization, as well as your readiness to manage the external environment in pursuit of your vision and long-term goals.

We hope this book will deepen your understanding of the planning and budgeting process and provide a valuable guide to assist you during your next budget cycle.

Introduction

If you are like most managers, you probably feel a heightened sense of anxiety at the start of the budgeting season. It represents one more item on an already full plate, and one more distraction from your real job of running the business. You dread the endless meetings, the difficult negotiations and, worst of all, the budget cuts that often put you on edge with key members of your team.

We concede that budgeting can be a stressful exercise. Top management must balance the needs of all stakeholders and their expectations of financial performance. There are never enough resources. The budget becomes a negotiation process between what you believe you can accomplish with the available resources and what your manager wants done. It can be frustrating and demoralizing for both you and your staff.

But there is good news! The budgeting process can be managed. The key to successful budgeting involves planning, organization, documentation, preparation, and follow-up.

A sound budget is based on a well-thought-out plan, with long-term and short-term objectives and accountability for results. The development of this plan requires time, effort, and commitment from all key players, but particularly from the senior management team. If they are not committed, your planning process will be flawed and so will your budget. The budget process also requires regular progress reviews and, most important, actions that will be determined based on those reviews to help you reach the desired end state.

To be successful, you should understand where your company is going and its short-term objectives for the next fiscal year.

Identify any environmental factors you need to address and analyze how well you are positioned to manage them. You'll also need to understand how your budget affects the organization's financial and operational performance. The budget is the financial quantification of the resources you need to run the business; therefore, any budgeting decisions will affect your organization, and ultimately be reflected in the financial results.

Each planning and budgeting cycle represents an opportunity for change. It is a chance to revisit the old and embrace the new. The budget is not something to fear on your "to do" list, but a time to reexamine who you are, what you do, and how you can use your resources more effectively. How you approach this process will determine your success in achieving your short-term and long-term objectives.

About This Book

This book will walk you through the fundamentals of planning and budgeting in 10 simple steps. Their essence can be summarized in one key learning objective: **Plan first, budget later.** These key steps will make the budgeting process less of a burden and more of an opportunity for you to understand and drive your business success. This book will help you understand how to work through and manage a budget and realize that preparing a budget is part of a larger, more complex process involving teamwork and management commitment to ensure a successful outcome.

Starting with a macro perspective, this book provides an overview of the planning and budgeting process and how it is typically structured within an organization. We discuss the functions of the process and the major elements of a strategic plan. We then move from this macro perspective to what interests you as a manager—how to prepare a sound budget and defend it to the next level of management. Our combined experience of more than 30 years in planning and budgeting will help you navigate this process successfully.

Chapter-by-Chapter Overview

Step 1: Know the purpose of planning and budgeting.

As you read through this step, think about your own company's planning and budgeting process. Does it fulfill all these functions? Where does it fall short? How can you help fix it?

Step 2: Know the planning and budgeting cycle.

This step defines and describes the elements of a strategic plan and discusses the importance of identifying roles and responsibilities, establishing accountability, and understanding critical interdependencies.

Step 3: Know the elements of an operating budget.

As a manager, you will be actively involved in the preparation of the operating budget for your areas of responsibility. You should understand where you fit into the big picture of your organization, and how your information gets rolled into the financial statements.

Step 4: Communicate budget requirements and obtain commitment.

This step is key and should be completed before you start developing your short-term plans, and definitely before you start calculating numbers. Remember, budgeting is not an exercise for the Lone Ranger!

Step 5: Analyze the operating environment for your areas of responsibility.

This analysis will provide your team with a shared understanding of the opportunities and threats in the external environment over which you may have limited or no control, and the strengths and weaknesses of your areas of responsibility to address them.

Step 6: Develop short-term objectives, strategies, and tactical plans.

Here we emphasize the use of SMART objectives (specific, measurable, attainable, realistic, and time-bound) and the identification of key metrics to measure your progress throughout the year.

Step 7: Prepare your departmental spending budget.

This step is probably what motivated you to buy this book. We explain how to quantify the resources you need in financial terms to implement your work plan and achieve your short-term objectives. We describe how to analyze the key activities of your department, determine staffing requirements, analyze your cost structure, and calculate major spending categories. We have also included a tool, "How to Estimate Your Departmental Spending," which summarizes common line items and suggests a possible estimation base to calculate the budgeted amount for each.

Step 8: Obtain approval for your budget.

This step is probably the most stressful part of the process. We explain the different levels of review and how to come to terms with the inevitable budget cuts. We also discuss how to manage the review process, as well as some dos and don'ts that will make the process less painful.

Step 9: Communicate plans and priority projects.

Similar to step 4, this step is about the communication process once your budget has been approved. We have participated in many budgeting exercises where budget cuts and performance expectations are not communicated back to the key players who have to execute the plans. This breakdown in communication can result in missed objectives, budget overruns, very unhappy managers, and frustrated employees.

Step 10: Review performance against plan and act!

This step completes the planning cycle and brings it full circle—you plan, budget, execute, and review. We show you how to analyze budget variances and monitor progress against your objectives. Most importantly, we emphasize the need to *act*! We have seen many managers analyze their budget variances month after month and do nothing. This action (yes, doing nothing is an action) defeats the purpose of analyzing your actual versus budgeted spending levels. Variance analysis should spur you to take the necessary actions to keep your organization financially and operationally on track. We end this step explaining the nature of the financial forecast, its role in the planning and budget cycle, and its importance.

This book will provide you with a valuable reference tool to plan, prepare, and defend a budget that is strategically aligned to your organization. We urge you to highlight key passages, earmark pages for quick review, and share it with new managers who have never participated in the budgeting process. Remember: A budget is the financial quantification of the resources you need to support the business objectives for the next fiscal year. Make sure you keep your eye on the ball as you go through this process. Happy budgeting!

Step 1

Know the Purpose of Planning and Budgeting

Overview

- Recognize the difference between planning and budgeting.
- Know the functions of a plan.
- Use the planning process to drive results.

You've just received the dreaded email from your finance department announcing the start of the budgeting process. You think of the countless meetings, the endless negotiations with your boss, budget cuts—stress, stress, and more stress. How can you survive with your sanity intact? There must be a way to make the process more manageable.

Budgeting will always be a painful process. It takes time and effort to develop plans for the upcoming year and estimate the resources required. It is particularly difficult when you are preparing your budget months in advance of the start of the fiscal year.

Your budget is part of a larger process called planning. It cannot be done in a vacuum and be must connected to the mission, vision, goals, and objectives of the organization. Planning is not something that is done once a year or once a quarter. Good planning requires constant revision and high involvement from operational managers. Those plans are translated into budgets and forecasts, which show the expected financial results of the proposed strategies.

The first step to successful budgeting is knowing the purpose of planning and budgeting in your organization. Let's start by explaining the difference between planning and budgeting, and how they are interrelated.

Recognize the Difference Between Planning and Budgeting

Planning involves identifying the goals and objectives for a specific time horizon and the specific strategies and action plans to achieve them. It should be based on a thorough analysis of the internal and external operating environment. These plans are eventually translated into budgets and forecasts, which are used to track and monitor performance.

The budget is a financial document that quantifies, in monetary terms, the action plans of the company over a short period of time, typically a year. Some companies have started to stretch the budget horizon beyond a year to 24–36 months. This requirement forces managers to think beyond a year as many strategies and action plans cannot be fully implemented in a 12-month period.

During the budgeting process, managers should strive to maximize the use of organizational resources aligned with the strategic direction. The budget is a means to an end, not an end in itself. Often, you can get so involved in crunching the numbers that you forget the strategies and action plans that are driving the numbers. You cannot cut a budget without affecting your plans for the year, unless you have sandbagged the numbers. *Sandbagging* is a commonly used term in the budgeting process whereby a manager overestimates the amount of spending required, which then allows for flexibility when budget cuts are requested. We do not recommend this approach and will explain why in later chapters.

Now that you understand the difference between planning and budgeting, let us review the reasons why companies plan.

Know the Functions of a Plan

Planning and budgeting require a large investment of time and resources. Why do companies invest such a significant, and often seemingly disproportionate, amount of resources in this effort? A well-thought-out plan serves several important functions within the organization.

Resource Allocation

The planning process forces you to think beyond the day to day and determine what resources are required to achieve your objectives. Resources include materials, people, equipment, facilities, and funding. These resources are quantified during the budgeting process. The budgeting process is when the rubber meets the road. It is the time to ask and answer some hard questions and determine if you must scale down your plans to meet management expectations.

POINTER

Questions to assess the adequacy of your resources:
- What resources do you need?
- What resources do you have?
- Are your resources properly aligned and allocated?
- Is there redundancy in your areas of responsibility or with another department or business unit?
- Can you do more with less?

Resource allocation is a key function of the planning process and allows the organization to evaluate if they have the right resources in place to support the business. This assessment may entail taking some resources away from you to give them to another priority area.

Spending Control

The budget establishes a control mechanism to ensure that you spend the money assigned according to the plan. Through the budgeting process, management authorizes an amount of money to achieve specific objectives. It is not a pot of money to spend as you please.

In well-managed organizations, you will be required to explain why you spent more or less than the planned amounts. You may also be required to incorporate any changes to the business environment in a financial forecast or identify specific actions you have taken to meet or beat the budget.

Communication and Coordination

The planning and budgeting process provides a unique opportunity to coordinate the efforts of various parts of the organization and minimize redundancy of functions and resources. In some organizations, the right hand does not know what the left hand is doing. During the planning process, you should share your plans with your peers to ensure that they are aligned and move the organization in the desired direction. Ideally, all members of the management team should be able to comment and provide feedback on the plans of other areas.

This communication is even more critical for support areas, such as facilities, human resources, finance, and information systems. We have seen projects grind to a halt because a key support area was not included in the planning and did not have the necessary budget.

POINTER

If you involve your team in planning and budget preparation, make sure you communicate the end result once the process is finished–for example, tell them what got approved, what didn't, and what was postponed, as well as the reasons for these decisions.

Finally, it is important to involve key members of your team in the planning and budgeting process. Your team may have critical information that you are unaware of and can assist you with the number crunching and data collection. This involvement will ensure their buy-in and provide you with some assurance that you have not overcommitted the organization.

Feedback

The planning process generally results in an annual budget you can use to monitor and evaluate your performance. The budget also provides a systematic mechanism to update the plan based on changing business conditions.

The budget is presented and reported in monetary terms. It measures *efficiency*, which is how the money was used by major spending category. However, it does not measure *effectiveness*—if the money spent achieved the stated objectives. Therefore, the budget should be tied to key performance measures that will allow you to evaluate if the resources consumed in your area are achieving the desired results. Some examples of performance measures may include units sold, units produced, labor hours per unit, overtime hours, customer complaints, percentage of on-time shipments, backorders, cost per unit, and cost per employee.

You should determine the important performance measures for your areas of responsibility and ensure that these are reported on a monthly or quarterly basis. Your revenue or spending levels may be right on target in monetary terms, but your performance measures may indicate that you are not achieving your objectives or that a problem is brewing on the horizon.

Simulations

The planning process allows you to perform simulations or "what-ifs" and understand the financial implications of your plans without playing them out in real life. You should build a financial model for your area based on key assumptions and change these assumptions to understand how they affect your budgeted amounts.

Simulations allow you to determine whether your plans are realistic or if you require more resources than the organization can afford. They will also help you identify areas of opportunity to bring your resources in line with management expectations. A robust financial model can help you foresee difficult situations and develop contingency plans *before* a crisis occurs.

External Demands

Do you ever wonder where senior management gets the financial information that they report to Wall Street or their bankers? You guessed it—the planning and budgeting process! Outsiders to your organization, such as Wall Street analysts, investors, and banks, require your company to provide information on its future direction. The accuracy of this information has implications for the prestige of the company in the investor community and, if publicly traded, can ultimately affect the stock price.

Budgets and forecasts are used to communicate regularly with external users of financial information. The planning and budgeting process culminates with the preparation of *proforma financial statements* that summarize the results of the company plans in monetary terms. Proforma financial statements are those prepared based on plans and assumptions about the internal and external environment. They usually include a balance sheet, an income statement, and statement of cash flows.

Use the Planning Process to Drive Results

The planning and budget process can be a powerful tool to drive business results if properly structured and managed. Now that you understand the functions of planning and budgeting in your organization, you should use this knowledge to identify or review how you can improve the process, either in your own area or for the organization as a whole. Some actions that you can take are:

- Identify the weak links and areas of opportunity in the process.
- Look for ways to eliminate redundancy and rework in your own area of responsibility or with other areas in the organization.
- Improve communications with your peers and subordinates. Understand their plans for the upcoming year and give them your feedback.
- Ensure you have adequate feedback mechanisms to raise a red alert when you deviate from the plan.
- Develop financial models to prepare for contingencies and budget cuts.

Use the budgeting self-assessment questionnaire in Worksheet 1-1 to help you evaluate your own budgeting process and identify areas for improvement.

The Next Step

The budget should never be a straitjacket that prevents you from doing what is right. The process should motivate you and your people to take the right course of action within the resource limitations of the organization and management expectations. We conclude with words of wisdom from Professors Charles Horngren and George Foster of Stanford University: "Changing conditions call for changes in plans. The budget must receive respect, but it should not prevent a manager from taking prudent action." Next, step 2 addresses the importance of understanding your organization's planning and budgeting cycle.

WORKSHEET 1-1
BUDGETING SELF-ASSESSMENT

Use this budgeting self-assessment questionnaire to help evaluate your budgeting process and identify areas of opportunity. If you answer no to any question, identify the actions that you can take to improve in this area.

Task	Yes	No	Actions Required
1. Do I know the organizational priorities and expectations for the budget?			
2. Did I establish my short-term plans and objectives before preparing the budget?			
3. Have I verified that these plans are aligned with management expectations?			
4. Have I discussed these plans with my direct reports and my boss?			
5. Do I know the plans of my peers or other critical areas of the organization that may affect me?			
6. Can I quantify the resources needed with the information I have?			
7. Do I know who I depend on for critical budgeting information?			
8. Do I know who depends on me for critical budget information?			
9. Have I defined the key financial and nonfinancial performance measures for my area?			
10. Is my budget based on a financial model in which I can easily change key assumptions?			
11. Do I have a systematic mechanism to monitor my actual performance against the plan on a monthly basis?			
12. Do I understand how to communicate changes to the budgeted plans and their potential financial impact?			

Step 2

Know the Planning and Budgeting Cycle

Overview

- Know the elements of the plan.
- Define the roles and responsibilities.
- Establish the timeline.
- Understand the interdependencies.

The *strategic plan,* also known as a *business plan,* is the foundation of the planning and budgeting cycle. Having discussed the importance of planning and budgeting in the previous chapter, we now turn to the description and definition of the various components of the business plan.

Let us say you are planning a vacation. You start from somewhere—say your home town—and you have a destination in mind, which is your goal. You proceed to select your method of transportation, what places you will visit, and what activities you will do during your stay. You'll need to know how much your vacation is going to cost and how you will pay for it. If, after running the numbers, you discover you cannot afford the vacation as planned, you will start looking for alternatives to reduce costs. Should you drive? Can you stay with family or friends? Do you need to find a less expensive destination within your means?

Planning your business is like planning a vacation. You need to establish what you want to accomplish, where your business is headed, how to get there, and what resources you require. The business plan provides a blueprint for your organization to understand where you come from, and what you want to achieve in the long run.

We will start by reviewing the six major elements of a business plan in the order that is most appropriate for the efficient preparation of a plan.

Know the Elements of the Plan

When we are dealing with a business organization, be it large or small, or even a not-for-profit entity, we need to understand what the organization will be doing. What is its purpose or reason for being? In terms of a business plan this sense of purpose is called a mission. A *mission* is the first and probably most critical element of your plan. It provides a framework to establish the long-term direction of the organization, and defines its core purpose: who you are, what you do, and who your target market is. The mission is not a marketing slogan; it is a well-thought-out statement that defines your company's purpose. Look at the following mission statements from Starbucks and Amazon:

- **Starbucks:** "To inspire and nurture the human spirit—one person, one cup, and one neighborhood at a time."
- **Amazon:** "To be the most customer centric company in the world, where people can find and discover anything they want to buy online."

What do these statements have in common? How are they different? Notice that the Starbucks statement does not even mention the word "coffee," which is their main product. They are more concerned with the customer experience. On the other hand, Amazon's statement is more direct in relation with their business of selling online, and yet they are also concerned about customer satisfaction.

Do you know your company's mission statement? If you don't, can you describe what your company does in a few words? Get a copy of your company's mission statement and see how close your perception is to that of top management. Did you mention your products, your customers, or your market? Is the mission clear? When you read the mission do you understand what the company does and who its target market is? The mission sets the starting point for our trip; it defines who we are and what we do. Now we need to define where we are headed.

The *vision* is the second element of a plan. It answers the question of where we want to be in the future. Many companies typically establish the vision with a 10-year time horizon. However, with the rapid speed of change in today's business environment, your vision could have a shorter timeframe.

A vision is a description of a desired future state and defines the organization's long-range direction and goals; it should support the mission of the entity. Vision statements should be inspirational and define a future state that you can measure. Some companies actually refer to beating specific competitors or capturing market share. Others are more general, but all portray a future that will guide the long-range strategies of your company. Take a look at the following vision statements from well-known organizations. These give you an idea of what a vision statement could look like:

- **Nike:** (in 1960s) "Crush Adidas."
- **ASPCA:** "That the United States is a humane community in which all animals are treated with respect and kindness."
- **Microsoft:** "A computer on every desk and in every home; all running Microsoft software."

It is important to note that vision statements can and will change over time. Once the company has achieved its vision, it must be changed. Major changes in your business model, products, or technology will also result in a need to review and change the vision. Are you clear on your company's vision? Can you articulate it in your own words? What are you doing today to move closer to the goal described in the vision?

The third element of a plan is the values. *Values* describe the basic principles that an organization holds dear. They should guide the actions of the company's management and employees, and their interactions with customers, suppliers, and other stakeholders. Hewlett Packard Company had a working philosophy known as "The HP Way." It referred to a set of values that every employee would follow in their daily dealings with customers, peers, colleagues, and vendors, as shown in Example 2-1. These values evolved over the years, but always with the same direction in mind: do the best job for your customers, treat employees with respect, and deal fairly with business partners and suppliers.

EXAMPLE 2-1
THE HP WAY

1. We have trust and respect for individuals.
2. We focus on a high level of achievement and contribution.
3. We conduct our business with uncompromising integrity.
4. We achieve our common objectives through teamwork.
5. We encourage flexibility and innovation.

Values may change over time, but companies that want to outshine their competitors must take the time to document and communicate their values within their organizations. HP went through a lot of changes over the last couple of decades: the spinoff of Agilent (the medical device group), the merger with Compaq and various other acquisitions, and most recently the split between HP Enterprise (services and servers) and HP Inc. (printers and computers). These reorganizations coupled with frequent changes in CEOs have led many to believe that HP has lost its "Way" and therefore one of its competitive advantages. Companies must ensure that changes in their values as well as long-term objectives are planned and revised to achieve continued success. Can you recall your company's values? Which ones affect you the most? Is there a particular value that you think is more important than another?

Now that we know who we are (mission), where we are headed (vision), and have guidelines on how to conduct ourselves (values), we are ready to examine the fourth element of the plan: goals and objectives.

A *goal* is a long-term outcome that the organization strives for. An *objective* supports a goal; it represents something specific that the organization wants to accomplish. Objectives can be long term or short term, but short-term objectives should pursue a long-term goal. Goals and objectives can be related to competitive positioning, technological leadership, profitability, productivity gains, talent development, or corporate image, among many other things.

Long-term objectives and goals are generally those that require more than a year to complete, usually three to five years. Short-term objectives are usually defined with a one- to two-year timeframe, and need to be established by the business units that are responsible for implementing them. Objectives should also be SMART: Specific, Measurable, Attainable, Realistic, and Time-Bound.

The use of objectives as a planning and measurement tool is not a new concept. Peter Drucker is known for his writings on management by objectives since the mid 1950s. By establishing specific goals and objectives, the company ensures that high priority areas are being worked on. Measuring progress against those objectives lets the company know how close it is to realizing its goal. The following are long-term objectives that project out five or 10 years and are not specific.

What Does SMART Stand For?

- **Specific** means that you know precisely what needs to be done.
- **Measurable** signifies that you can ascertain when the objective has been achieved.
- **Attainable** means the objective can be accomplished.
- **Realistic** implies that you have considered other factors, such as time and resources, in establishing the objective.
- **Time-bound** indicates that there is a deadline when the objective must be completed.

- Generic example:
  - "To exceed $15 million in gross revenue in the next 10 years"

- **Procter and Gamble's long-term objectives (P&G 2018):**
  - Grow Organic Sales
  - Grow Organic Volume
  - Grow Core Earnings Per Share
  - Improve Adjusted Cash Flow Productivity

Obviously, the larger the organization, the more resources that can be assigned to a given objective. Large companies like Facebook or Apple can have multiple, far-reaching objectives, while smaller companies will generally have a fewer areas of focus within the limits of their resources. The important lesson is that you must clearly define and communicate your goals and objectives throughout the organization. This knowledge will help managers and employees understand and differentiate between those activities that are key to the organization and those that do not move the company toward its future state. Can you mention the key goals and objectives that guide your organization toward its vision?

Once everyone is on board with the goals and objectives, it's time to develop the fifth element of the plan: the strategies. *Strategies* are mid- to long-term plans defined for a specific period, usually two to five years. They must support the company mission, vision, goals, and objectives.

Strategies answer the question: How do we plan to achieve our objectives? They are usually stated in general terms, such as identify cost reduction opportunities, open new channels of distribution, or renew our physical infrastructure.

The sixth element of a plan is *action plans,* also known as *tactical plans.* Each plan should be aligned with a strategy and describe the specific actions the organization will take to achieve its objectives within the established timeframe. They should tell you who, what, and when. They are individual activities or tasks, with assigned responsibilities, metrics, and deadlines. Managers should also identify key performance measures that provide critical feedback mechanisms to evaluate the effectiveness of these short-term plans. Figure 2-1 summarizes the six elements of the strategic plan and the sequence in which they should be prepared.

FIGURE 2-1

ELEMENTS OF A STRATEGIC PLAN

MISSION — Who are we? What do we do? What values are important to us?

VISION — Where are we going? What does our future state look like?

VALUES — How do we deal with customers, employees, and others?

GOALS & OBJECTIVES — What is the expected outcome?

STRATEGIES — How do we plan to achieve our objectives?

ACTION PLANS — What specific actions are we going to take?

Adapted from Oliver (2017).

STEP 2

We will end this section of plan elements by emphasizing that strategic planning is everyone's responsibility. At each level of the organization, managers make short-term and long-term plans. Although the scope of their decisions may vary, each level must consider the goals, objectives, and priorities of top management, as well as those of their immediate boss. The corporate mission, vision, and values are generally developed at higher levels in the organization, while the goal, objectives, strategies, and action plans are developed at the organization's lower levels. Depending on the size of the organization, there may be several layers of strategies, all nesting together and working toward the same goals.

Define the Roles and Responsibilities

A key part of understanding your planning and budgeting cycle is to be clear on the roles and responsibilities of everyone involved in the process. You need to ensure that you identify who is responsible and who is accountable. This identification process is important because not only will the budgeting tasks be carried out by different people in the organization, but often the tasks are shared or interdependent, as we will see later in this chapter.

What is the difference between responsibility and accountability? We will provide some classic definitions of these terms, but the important lesson is that each member of the organization must understand what their role is, and how they can affect the outcome of the process and the end product.

Responsibility refers to the ability and obligation to carry out a given task. It is assigned explicitly to someone to ensure the work gets done. *Accountability* is a condition where employees are expected to take ownership of their actions and answer for their decisions. Ultimately, they will take the blame for any work that is not done right. Only one person should be held accountable for an action and this person should agree that they are accountable. Typically, this person is a manager or project leader.

In structuring your budgeting team, it is essential that all team members are fully informed, agree on who is responsible for what, and determine who has the authority to make any critical decisions. Figure 2-2 shows an RACI Matrix, which is a tool used to document this responsibility structure.

FIGURE 2-2
THE RACI MATRIX

- **Responsible:** Who has been assigned to get the job done?
- **Accountable:** Who has ownership for this task?
- **Consulted:** Who needs to provide feedback or input?
- **Informed:** Who needs to know?

This matrix is basically a spreadsheet with the detail of the tasks, activities, and the team members that will be involved in the budgeting process. For each key task, you identify who is responsible or accountable, and who needs to be consulted or simply informed.

Establish the Timeline

As we have seen, the planning process, which must precede the budget preparation, can be quite complex and requires the involvement and commitment of many people in the organization. Therefore, a clear and well-communicated timeline is essential to the successful completion of this process. Depending on the size of your company, the process can take from a few days to five or six months.

If the strategic planning portion of the process (mission, vision, goals) has already occurred, you will need to establish a schedule that includes the following milestones:

- Review mission, vision, and objectives with your team.
- Discuss areas of influence and define which objectives your function will be working on.
- Establish roles and responsibilities and obtain buy-in from team members.
- Agree on assumptions to be used in the plan.
- Agree on deadlines for work and progress review.
- Develop individual and consolidated budgets.
- Prepare for top management review.
- Allow time to incorporate revisions into the final budget.
- Establish progress review schedule to compare actual to budgeted results.

As you can imagine, there will be lots of meetings and lots of work to be done in between. Management must ensure not only that the right people are participating in the process, but also that the day-to-day work is still being taken care of. This duality is why people hate the budgeting season: They must take time out of their busy schedules to plan and budget, but still "keep the plane flying."

POINTER

How to Minimize Meeting Waste
1. Plan and communicate meetings in advance.
2. Have a fixed start and end time.
3. State the objective of the meeting
4. Publish an agenda.
5. State the expected outcomes of the meeting.

Some managers believe that meetings are a colossal waste of time. To lessen the impact of wasted meeting time, we suggest that meetings be planned and communicated in advance, have a fixed start and end time, and have very clear agenda with specific objectives.

These meetings should not be optional. If you are responsible for a specific activity or task, you must attend and your work must be completed unless some major, unforeseen catastrophe hits your facility, like a fire, an earthquake, a hurricane . . . well, you get the picture. Lack of attendance should have consequences, and senior management must make sure their teams know that these meetings are a high priority.

Interdependencies

By now it should be clear that the budgeting process is not simply a financial exercise. Although the end result is generally expressed in numbers, be it your spending budget, sales revenue, or net profit, budget preparation is not possible without the coordinated efforts of all members of the organization. For example, the human resources department may suggest that you make changes to your salary structure or add a new benefit to attract and retain the best employees. This action, of course, costs money and will affect every department in the organization. Senior management may require you to improve process efficiency to cover the additional cost. This action may require the purchase of additional equipment, which in turn may require making major building improvements, and so it goes on.

You start getting the picture that a budget cannot be done in a vacuum, managers must bring their piece of the puzzle to the game, and to win, everyone must be on the same page. Smaller organizations may have an easier time at this process, with the finance person doing all the number crunching. Even then, this individual must be aware of what is going on in the organization to prepare a meaningful budget that can guide the actions of the management team.

Next Step

This step explains the critical components of a good planning and budgeting process. Worksheet 2-1 provides a self-assessment tool that will help you ascertain your knowledge of the process in your company. To further understand your role in the big picture, step 3 focuses on the elements of the operating budget.

WORKSHEET 2-1
HOW WELL DO YOU KNOW YOUR PLANNING PROCESS?

Here is a list of questions to evaluate your knowledge of the planning cycle in your company. This worksheet will help you identify the knowledge gaps and what additional information you need to have a more thorough understanding of the process.

Question	Your Answer
What is your company's year-end reporting date?	
When are your company's budgets due?	
Do you have a copy of your company's mission and vision statements?	
When was the last time your mission and vision statements were reviewed or shared with managers and employees?	
Who is responsible for the annual budget?	
Have you ever participated in the budgeting process?	
Is there a formal schedule for the planning process? Has it been shared or reviewed by you?	
Do you have monthly or quarterly meetings to review budget to actual?	
What was last year's most significant accomplishment? Was it related to the major objectives or vision?	
Is your company expected to grow or suffer significant changes in the coming years?	

Step 3

Know the Elements of an Operating Budget

Overview

- Understand what an operating budget is.
- Know how each element is calculated.
- Recognize the importance of the headcount plan.
- Understand the capital budget and its relationship to the operating budget.

Putting together the operating budget is like assembling a jigsaw puzzle. Different parts of the organization are responsible for pieces of this puzzle, which when added together form a financial representation of the plans and key initiatives for the upcoming year. The budget will be the basis for communicating up and down the organizational hierarchy and set management expectations of future financial performance to shareholders, investors, bankers, and other interested parties.

How do you fit into this larger picture? What piece of the budget are you responsible for and how should it be put together? In this step, we will discuss the operating budget, how it differs from a financial budget, and the major elements that compose it.

What Is an Operating Budget?

The *operating budget* is a financial representation of the organization's short-term plans across all functions. It is composed of many different pieces—including the income statement and all supporting budget schedules—which come together to summarize the expected financial performance of the organization.

The *financial budget* shows the impact of the operating plans, financing, and capital expenditure decisions on the organization's cash flow and financial performance. It consists of the capital budget, the cash budget, and the budgeted financial statements. It is prepared by the finance team, with some involvement from nonfinancial managers, particularly with respect to inventory and capital investments.

As a nonfinancial manager, supervisor, or key employee, you will be actively involved in the preparation of the operating budget. You will develop the business strategies and define short-term plans for your areas of responsibility. You will also need to estimate the resources required to meet these plans and determine the key assumptions that underlie the budgeted amounts. You'll prepare and review the numbers that will ultimately be summarized in a budgeted income statement for top management approval.

The Basic Financial Statements

- **The balance sheet** captures an image of the financial condition of your company at a specific point in time. It shows the economic resources of the organization and claims against these resources as of a particular date.
- **The income statement** measures the financial performance of the organization over a period of time.
- **The statement of cash flows** details the sources and uses of cash over the same period of time as the income statement. It shows how the cash position of the company changed from one period to the next.

Elements of an Operating Budget

The operating budget is summarized in the three major elements of the income statement: sales, cost of sales, and operating expenses. Figure 3-1 shows the major elements of an operating budget and how they are summarized in the income statement. Next we will explain how to build the operating budget and how you can calculate each major element.

FIGURE 3-1
HOW THE OPERATING BUDGET TIES TO THE INCOME STATEMENT

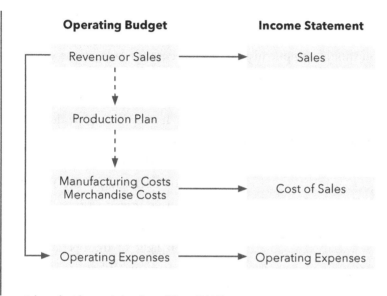

Adapted with permission from Oliver (2017).

Revenue or Sales

To be able to spend money, you must first have money to spend. The *revenue or sales budget* represents the monetary value of the product and services that you will provide your customer for the budget period. It is the fundamental building block of the operating budget. It drives the resource allocation of other areas, such as manufacturing and sales, and also determines the funds that will be available to support investments in R&D and infrastructure. The sales budget should support your strategic direction and it will be driven by the major assumptions that should be defined prior to the start of any actual budget calculations.

Past sales performance provides a reasonable starting point for estimating future sales, and is hard data you can use to validate or challenge your assumptions. If historical data are not available, you must gather it from other sources, such as your own sales force, industry reports, and trade associations. As you gather sales data, you should determine what information is available and for what time periods. Often, the sales data are available, but not accessible or summarized in a useful manner. You may have to reorganize the available data or design new reports.

You should compile historical sales data for at least one year. This timeframe will allow you to identify seasonal trends and nonrecurring items, such as special orders or promotions that should not be considered in the budget projections. It may also provide important information about pricing behavior and how your customers responded to price increases or decreases, either from you or your competitors.

Sales data should be analyzed in light of the operating environment: What is the trend? Are sales increasing or decreasing? Is your industry in a stage of high growth? Is it mature or stagnant? What external factors—such as a rise in interest rates, environmental regulations, seasonal epidemics, or a change in demographics—may affect your sales? Finally, you also need to consider the expectations of outside stakeholders, such as bankers, investors, and shareholders, whom you should have identified prior to the start of the budgeting process.

POINTER

There are a few key assumptions you need to consider when budgeting revenue or sales:

- **What product or services do you intend to sell?** Do you have new products that may cannibalize your existing sales? Are there products that will be discontinued?
- **Who is your target market?** Are there market segments you wish to enter? Is this market growing or shrinking?
- **What sales channels do you use to distribute your product?** Are there new sales channels available or are there other sales channels you should consider?
- **At what price should you sell your products or services?** How does customer demand respond to price changes?

Now that you have analyzed all your sales data, how do you go about preparing the actual budgeted dollars? In its simplest form, the sales budget multiplies the estimated sales volume based on your assumptions by an average price, as shown in Example 3-1.

EXAMPLE 3-1
A SIMPLE SALES BUDGET

Product	Budget		
	Volume (units) [1]	Price per unit [2]	Sales [1] x [2]
A	10,000	$25	$250,000
B	50,000	$10	$500,000
Total Budgeted Sales			$750,000

The sales volume should be expressed in one or more tangible measures, which should tie the financial results directly to the heart of your business. Each organization must determine the appropriate measures to use as the basis for estimating revenue. In manufacturing organizations, this basis is typically units sold per period. In service organizations, it can be a variety of measures depending on the services provided—for example, labor hours, customers, orders, patient hours, or square footage.

In the final analysis, budgeting sales is an art, not a science. After the numbers are crunched, you will probably need to adjust the sales figures up or down, depending on what number you feel comfortable committing to and the expectations of the next level of management. However, there can be unforeseen consequences for your organization. If your budgeted sales are too high, you may end up with excess capacity—too many people and underutilized facilities. This excess capacity has a cost, which will negatively affect net income or the "bottom line." The reverse is also true: Underestimating sales will result in not having enough capacity—people, equipment, or facilities—to meet customer demand, resulting in lost sales or increased costs, again negatively affecting the bottom line.

Note that all assumptions used to prepare the sales budget and any qualitative adjustments made by management should be documented. If sales do not materialize as planned, you will be able to trace these differences to actual decisions made during the planning process. This understanding can help you assign responsibility and improve the preparation of sales budgets in the future.

The sales budget is the first step in building an operating budget. It puts an upper limit on the amount of resources available for the upcoming year. If sales are growing, there will be more money to spend. If sales are stagnant or shrinking, it is time to put on the brakes. Once the sales budget is finalized, each department or area can start estimating the level of resources required to meet the company objectives. This resource allocation process occurs throughout the organization. Manufacturing entities, however, must translate the sales budget into a production plan before they can estimate their resource requirements for the upcoming year.

The Production Plan

The *production plan* details the quantities of each major product that will be manufactured during the year and is expressed in a tangible unit of measure, such as units, pounds, gallons, or tablets. Managers use the production plan to estimate the resources required in the manufacturing operations to achieve the planned volume levels. These resources are usually budgeted by department or work center and are the basis for calculating manufacturing costs.

Service organizations generally do not prepare a production plan. However, they should perform some type of capacity planning to ensure they have the resources in place to meet customer demands. That would entail estimating the service levels or possibly the number of customers you want to reach within the budget period.

Production Costs

Production or manufacturing costs consist of three major elements: direct materials, direct labor, and overhead. *Direct materials costs* typically include the purchase cost of raw materials, subassemblies, and packaging components, plus any other costs incurred to get the items into inventory, such as in-bound freight, broker fees, and in-transit insurance. You should be able to trace materials directly to the item being produced. Miscellaneous supplies, such as nuts, tools, and cleaning articles, are not included in these costs.

Direct materials costs are based on a *bill of materials (BOM)*, which is a listing of the components and the quantities required to build a product. It can be as simple as an Excel spreadsheet or part of a formal *enterprise resource planning* (ERP) system. Example 3-2 shows a typical BOM—the item number of each component, its description, the unit of measure, and the quantity required to manufacture the end product.

EXAMPLE 3-2
WHAT DOES A BOM LOOK LIKE?

Product Number: 99-223
Description: Bottle of 30 mg tablets

Item Number	Description	Unit of Measure	Quantity per Unit
32-105	Tablet, 30 mg	each	500
32-223	Bottle	each	1
32-334	Cap	each	1
33-060	Label	each	1
15-641	Cotton puff	each	1

If you work in production, engineering, or materials management, you may be asked to review the BOM at least once a year. Remember, the BOM drives inventory purchases based on the production plan. An inaccurate BOM may create material shortages during the year, which could stop a production line or result in unanticipated freight charges. Therefore, if you are charged with this responsibility, it is not something to take lightly.

Items in the BOM are multiplied by their unit cost and then added together to obtain the direct materials cost per unit of measure (UM).

Individuals who work in the purchasing or procurement function are usually responsible for providing the unit cost of the purchased components, such as raw materials, packaging, or outsourced intermediate products. If you work in these functions it is important to not only look at historical data, but take into consideration any upcoming vendor negotiations or forecasted increases of key commodities (such as oil, natural gas, wheat, and corn) that affect the cost of your purchases.

Direct Labor

Direct labor costs represent the cost of those employees who manufacture or assemble a product. These costs generally include base wages, payroll taxes, fringe benefits, overtime, and any other type of special compensation, such as shift differentials and productivity bonuses.

Direct labor costs are budgeted in production work centers and assigned to products based on a labor rate calculated for the work center and the estimated labor hours required to manufacture the product. The estimated labor hours are multiplied by the direct labor rate to obtain the direct labor costs per unit. The direct labor rate can be an average rate for all production areas or a specific labor rate for each manufacturing cost center.

Production managers or industrial engineers are typically responsible for setting and reviewing time standards. We recommend that these standards be updated at least once a year during the budgeting process. Obsolete time standards can wreak havoc on your capacity planning, and may result in significant cost variances.

Production Overhead

Production overhead, also known as *manufacturing or factory overhead,* consists of all manufacturing costs other than direct labor or materials. These costs may include management and supervisory salaries, equipment and building maintenance, production supplies, depreciation, utilities, rent, and allocated costs.

Manufacturing overhead costs are generally common to more than one product and must be assigned in a reasonable manner. The calculation of the overhead costs per unit is typically performed by the finance department and is beyond the scope of this book. Suffice to say, inaccurate time standards can also affect the manufacturing overhead costs that are assigned to a product.

Calculating Production Costs

Once the information required to calculate each cost element is finalized, you can start computing the manufacturing cost per unit. This process, called the cost *rollup*, is the sum of the direct materials, direct labor, and overhead costs discussed earlier. It is usually performed by the finance team, either automatically through the company's ERP system or manually using a spreadsheet application. Your responsibility as a manager is to review the output of this process and ensure that it makes sense for your operations. If the cost of a product seems wrong, challenge the cost calculation and review the underlying data with finance.

Cost of Sales

Cost of sales is calculated by multiplying the production cost per unit for each product by its budgeted sales volume. Again, this process is usually done automatically by your ERP system or the finance department in a spreadsheet application. Organizations that do not have manufacturing costs per unit, due to the nature of their business, can estimate cost of sales as a percentage of revenue based on historical data and management's assessment of the operating environment for the next fiscal year.

Operating Expenses

Operating expenses are usually budgeted by department, and include such departments as research and development, sales and marketing, and general and administrative expenses. Headcount-related costs account for a significant portion of these expenses. We will discuss the importance of the headcount plan in the next section. Operating expenses are budgeted at the discretion of the department manager using their experience to estimate the resources required to accomplish the plans for the next fiscal year.

Now let us discuss two other important components that are usually required as part of an operating budget: the headcount plan and the capital budget.

Headcount Plan

Your operating budget should be accompanied by a *headcount plan,* which details the current and future staffing requirements of your organization by business unit, department, and job classification. The headcount plan underlies one of the most significant expenses of the operating budget: the cost of your employees. It not only drives the budgeted wages and salaries of the organization, but also payroll taxes, fringe benefits, and other labor-related expenses, such as recruitment, training, and travel. In many organizations, headcount represents 60 to 70 percent of departmental spending. If you keep headcount under control, you will have better control of your spending levels.

The presentation of the headcount plan will vary according to the management reporting needs of each organization. Typically, it is presented by business unit and department, and classifies employees into three major groups: managerial and supervisory staff, technical and skilled professionals, and hourly employees. We will return to the headcount plan in step 7, where preparation of the departmental budget is described in more detail.

The Capital Budget

In addition to a headcount plan, you may be required to submit a *capital budget,* which consists of projects that require a significant disbursement of funds and have a long-term impact on the organization. It may include investments in land, buildings, machinery, equipment, vehicles, and information systems, among many others. In larger corporations, company policies provide clear guidelines as to when a project should be classified as a capital investment. In smaller companies, however, it may be dictated by the owners or senior management, or the applicable tax guidelines.

Capital Budgeting Definitions

- **Capital asset.** An economic resource that provides benefits to the organization over one or more years. It is classified as a fixed asset on the balance sheet. These assets are depreciated over their estimated useful life.
- **Depreciation.** A systematic method of charging the cost of an asset over its estimated useful life to different accounting periods.
- **Capital budget.** A structured plan for authorizing capital expenditures for the next fiscal year. It includes the list of approved capital investments and their related costs.
- **Capital appropriation request.** A form used to formally initiate and receive approval for a capital investment project. As a general rule, this project should have been included in the capital budget.

The capital budget is an integral part of the annual budgeting process and an important first step in the capital investment decision. It provides the organization with a structured plan for authorizing capital expenditures during the year, based on the strategic objectives of the organization. Because capital investment decisions can affect the stability, flexibility, and costs of the organization, they should be reviewed with the same rigor as the headcount plan and departmental spending budgets.

As a manager, you will be required to submit more than just a list of your capital projects. Each project will require a business justification, which is usually a form that you have to fill out for every capital project included in the budget, as shown in Example 3-3.

The Next Step

This step provided an overview of the major elements of the operating budget so that you can understand where you fit in the big picture. It is important that you identify what parts of the budget you are responsible for and how you affect others in this process. Armed with this knowledge, you are now ready to proceed to step 4, how to communicate the budget requirements to your team and obtain their commitment.

Example 3-3
An Example of Capital Budget Request Form

Requestor	Name of the department manager or project champion
Department	Name of the department where the asset will reside
Project Description	Description of the proposed project in plain and simple language. Avoid the use of technical jargon!
Business Justification	How does this project align with the long-term direction of the organization? What key strategy or initiative does it support? Why must it be started next year?
Project Costs	Detail all the costs of the project, including any incremental operating expenses. Capital costs are expenditures that will be capitalized as a fixed asset on the balance sheet and will be charged to the income statement over its useful life. Operating expenses are incremental expenditures that will not be capitalized, but should be included in the operating budget of your department, for example incremental headcount, maintenance contracts, repair costs, and post-implementation training. These costs would not be incurred if the project is not approved.
Expected Benefits	Address the expected benefits. What expected benefits will be obtained from this investment? Is it a compliance issue? Will it increase quality, reduce costs, or improve customer service? A financial evaluation may be required, although some companies postpone this analysis until a formal capital appropriation request is submitted.
Risks	Detail any associated risks. This will provide management with a better understanding of the financial and operational uncertainties involved with this project.

Step 4

Communicate Budget Requirements and Obtain Commitment

Overview
- Identify who needs to be involved.
- Determine the information needed.
- Meet with your team.
- Review the budget timeline.
- Get buy-in from your team.

You have been given your marching orders. Top management has communicated their expectations and the key priorities for the next fiscal year. However, before you can start preparing the budget for your areas of responsibility, you should assemble the team that will be involved in its preparation.

Rarely do managers have all the information required to prepare the budget for their areas of responsibility. Therefore, you need to identify the key individuals who should be involved in the budgeting process for your areas, and communicate expectations, priorities, and deadlines. Communication is a key element of any successful budgeting process. The communication flow should involve not only the next level of management for your areas of responsibility, but also any key members of your team, even if they do not have management or supervisory responsibilities. It should also include other areas outside your span of control that you may need to involve in your budgeting process.

Who Needs to Get Involved?

In Step 3, we discussed the elements of an operating budget. Those elements for which you are responsible will determine who needs to be involved. The information required may be as simple submitting a departmental spending budget and headcount plan, or as complex as preparing the sales budget or production plan, evaluating major acquisitions or mergers, budgeting key strategic initiatives across the organization, or capital investments.

Your team can help you analyze the internal and external operating environment, develop the short-term objectives and action plans for your areas of responsibility, and estimate the budgeted amounts. If you are the head of a business unit, at a minimum you should involve all your direct reports. If you are a department manager, you should involve your supervisors and any key professional employees who may add value to the process. Your team members should be individuals who have key information or the responsibility to make decisions that will affect the operations over the budget period. These decisions may include people management, customer interactions, asset purchases, and performance goal setting.

Look for people with business acumen who are willing to challenge assumptions and are not afraid to speak their minds. This diversity of thought will produce a more robust plan, because the team will clearly think through risks and opportunities. In addition to members of your team, you may want to involve key support areas such as facilities, engineering, human resources, and finance. The financial analyst can help you with the number crunching, and ensure your numbers pass muster with the finance staff. The human resources specialist can help you identify and resolve any potential people issues, whether it be recruiting, training, or performance evaluations. Engineering and facilities can help you identify cost improvement opportunities, potential safety hazards, and other key issues related to facilities and process management.

What Information Is Needed and Who Will Provide It?

A successful budgeting process requires a clear understanding of the information that your team needs before you start crunching the numbers. Based on the budget requirements for your areas of responsibility, you should prepare a list of the information that you will need from your own or other areas to meet the budget deadlines.

Imagine trying to prepare your budget without having a finalized sales plan. You would not know the upper limits of spending or what your areas need to do to meet the sales objectives. So, having a sales plan is one of the first steps in the budgeting process. Similarly, you should look for other interdependencies. Are you responsible for setting the estimated costs of materials and supplies? Are you responsible for reviewing the amount of material required for a product or service and updating the enterprise resource planning (ERP) system accordingly? Are you responsible for any key strategic initiative that may require a capital investment and the support of other areas?

You may also need to disclose other pieces of information in preparation for the budget exercise, such as expected salary increases, the upper limit on productivity bonuses, and any other changes to employee benefits. Your team should clearly understand management expectations. Is management expecting productivity improvements or a specific percent reduction in spending? If so, what actions do you plan to take and how will the results be incorporated into the budget? Once you and your team have discussed and itemized the information required to prepare the budget or give input to other areas, you should summarize it in a list and make it available to everyone.

It is imperative that you ask the right people to give you the information you need to build your budget or provide input to other areas. They should have a strong grasp of the business issues and how these should be addressed. You should not assign budgeting responsibilities to a rookie! In Tool 4-1 you'll find some suggestions about information you may need to complete the budget process, as well as the departments responsible for providing it.

Tool 4-1

Information required for your budget process

Information	Responsibility
1. The budget calendar with assigned areas of responsibilities and key due dates.	Finance
2. Any guidelines, procedures, and templates required by the finance department.	Finance
3. Management guidelines and key assumptions for the budget horizon.	Senior Management
4. A copy of your organization's strategic plan or any whitepaper that sets the strategic direction for the company or your business unit.	Management
5. Analysis of the external operating environment.	Various
6. Key strategic initiatives, capacity expansions, or facilities closures.	Planning
7. New product or services or the discontinuation of existing products or services.	Sales and Marketing
8. Historical sales trends and volumes by geographic region.	Sales and Marketing
9. Competitive analysis.	Planning Department
10. Forecasted sales volume for the budget period by market, product, service, and geographical region.	Sales
11. Production plan by market, products, and geographic region.	Planning
12. Forecasted cost of materials and supplies used to manufacture a product or provide a service.	Procurement

Once you have identified and documented the first draft of required information and assigned responsibilities to your team, you're ready for the next step: the budget kick-off meeting.

Meet With Your Team

You are finally ready to start the dreaded budget meetings. Many managers believe that these meetings are a waste of their time, affecting their day-to-day responsibilities. Therefore, it should be your goal to make these meetings as painless as possible and ensure participants understand the importance of the budget process and how it will help them manage the business. To make the most of the budget meetings (note the use of the plural as there will be more than one), you must be prepared and organized. Review Tool 4-2 for tips on how to minimize budget meeting waste, which can also be used for any type of meeting. Remember to always start and end meetings on time. Share the meeting schedule so team members can allocate enough time to complete the tasks assigned and avoid conflicts.

One of the main functions of the planning process, as we mentioned in step 1, is to ensure that everyone is on the same page. The budget kick-off meeting should start with a presentation or review of the business plan goals. What is the "big picture"? Where is the company headed? Are sales growing, stagnant, or in decline? Are we expecting to be more profitable, or are we struggling and need to reduce costs or improve productivity to survive? What are the short- and long-term goals of the organization?

In this meeting, you should clarify management's expectations about the result of this process. Do they expect major cost or spending reductions from last year? Is the company in a growth mode, which will require hiring and training new employees? If there are external factors at play, these should be identified too. A discussion on external factors may serve as the starting point for the operating environment analysis, which we will discuss further in step 5. It is also a good time to review any confidentiality issues—what can or cannot be shared with people who are not on the team.

Finally, you should use the kick-off meeting to plan for future budget meetings so the team can block their agendas. Attendance at future meetings should be compulsory with no excuses. Establish meeting ground rules, such as no texting or phone use, to ensure everyone stays focused during the discussions. In these meetings, your team will be analyzing the internal and external operating environment (step 5) and developing the short-term objectives, strategies, and action plans (step 6) that will underlie the budgeted amounts for your areas of responsibility.

TOOL 4-2
HOW TO MINIMIZE BUDGET MEETING WASTE

Use the following tips to help avoid meeting waste:
- Have fixed days for budget meetings with an established start and end time.
- Develop and communicate a detailed agenda for each meeting, including the meeting's purpose and expected outcomes.
- Include only members of the team who are essential. Do not invite everybody! Attendance should be compulsory with no excuses.
- Email important information to the team prior to the meeting. Make sure members know they must be prepared.
- Establish ground rules at the start of the meeting.
- Stay on topic and take notes.
- Assign a scribe to monitor the time and document decisions. Ensure any items placed in a "parking lot" for future discussion are either resolved in the meeting or placed on the agenda for the next meeting.
- Define action plans, persons responsible, and expected completion or review dates.
- Publish meeting notes 24 to 48 hours after the meeting. Clearly assign the responsibility for preparing and distributing these notes.
- Follow up on commitments and open action items at the start of the next meeting. Be sure to include these in the agenda.

Review the Budgeting Timeline and Critical Due Dates

Every team member needs to be clear on what is required of them and when each task must be completed for your budget process to be successful. Make sure you finalize a list of deliverables, the people responsible for their completion, and the timing of the budget-related activities during the kick-off meeting.

There are many ways you can plan and document your activities and progress. PERT (program evaluation and review technique) and CPM (critical path method) are the most common; you can find more information about them on the Internet, including software applications to manage the process. These methods summarize the steps in chronological order, define responsibilities and deadlines, and identify the critical items that must be finished before starting another task. For example, you need to complete the sales plan and inventory requirements before you can complete the production plan. You need to complete the production plan before completing the equipment and people plans. By identifying and documenting these relationships, you can build a timeline of which parts to complete before other areas complete their parts of the plan. This process helps your team understand the interdependencies with other areas and how the timeline may be at risk if someone fails to deliver according to plan. Identifying these tasks and establishing achievable deadlines is key to the successful completion of a budgeting exercise.

In the kick-off meeting, you should also identify whether your team is responsible for any key company initiatives and determine how to address these in your plan. Are you the project champion? Do you need to support one or more initiatives? What type of support is required? Do you need to budget incremental resources, such as headcount, travel, or equipment? How will they affect the budget? Do you need additional information to plan and budget these initiatives? Make sure you provide enough time for gathering information from other areas. Obtaining this information may be a challenge because the people who have it are not under your direct control and may have other directives and priorities. Scheduling a meeting with these people may be a more effective way to obtain the required information in a timely manner.

Get Buy-in and Commitment From Your Team

Before you finish the kick-off meeting and everyone runs off to their "real jobs," you need to make sure they are all committed to the tasks ahead and the schedule. You not only need a positive response from all the team members but also need to make sure they are all aligned with the company goals and objectives. Example 4-1 shows a sample meeting schedule.

EXAMPLE 4-1
SAMPLE MEETING SCHEDULE

- **Management kick-off meeting.** Present mission, vision, and objectives; define timeline and assign roles and responsibilities; and hold a question and answer period.
- **First meeting.** Agree on which objectives to address and discuss any proposed changes.
- **Second meeting.** Agree on assumptions and present sales or production plans and major projects to work on.
- **Third meeting.** Managers present action plans and proposed performance measures. Agree on milestones for first pass budget.
- **Fourth meeting.** The manager who is responsible for the budget reviews the first pass with finance.
- **Fifth meeting.** Present the first pass budget to team members and discuss any revisions or required budget cuts.
- **Budget review meeting.** Present the preliminary budget to next level management.
- **Second budget review meeting.** If necessary, present the revised budget, which incorporates the changes required by next-level management.
- **Present final budget to top management.** Be prepared; you may have to attend more meetings as the budget moves up and down the corporate hierarchy.

Make sure you, as the leader, bring a positive, energizing message to the first meeting, because it will set the tone for the entire process. You also need to identify roadblocks or concerns that may hinder your ability to meet the established deadlines. If the issues raised are outside your span of control, make a commitment to your team to work with the next level of management.

Keep the communication flow open and transparent. During this process, you want your team to believe that they are in a safe environment, where they can bring problems and concerns to the table without fear of negative consequences. The presence of a human resources representative or an experienced facilitator can help keep discussions on track and minimize finger pointing and destructive group dynamics.

The Next Step

In this step, we highlighted the importance of communication as a key element of any successful budgeting exercise. You need to communicate management expectations, priorities, and deadlines to your team and get their buy-in and commitment to this process. Communication will continue to be important as you start analyzing the internal and external operating environment and developing your short-term plans. You may also be required to involve other individuals who are not part of the core team or work in areas outside your span of control. Establishing the communication and collaboration mechanisms from the start will ease the path to completion and minimize the wear and tear on your team members' psyche. Tool 4-3 provides additional guidance to ensure a smoother and more effective budget process.

Tool 4-3
Guidelines for a Smoother Budgeting Process

1. Obtain copies of the current mission, vision, and objectives statements.
2. Define team members and set up a kick-off meeting to review the current mission, vision, and objectives.
3. Establish required due dates for the budget preparation and review the process.
4. Discuss organizational priorities, key initiatives, short-term objectives, and expense guidelines with the team members.
5. Get buy-in from the team on due dates and the guidelines.
6. Establish an RACI matrix so everyone is clear on expectations and responsibilities.
7. Define meeting rules, dates, timelines, and preparedness, including who would be an acceptable replacement if a team member must be absent.
8. Identify who has final accountability for the budget. The buck stops here!
9. Discuss the process for clearing conflicting activities—budgeting versus day-to-day operations.
10. Communicate, communicate, communicate!

Step 5

Analyze the Operating Environment for Your Areas of Responsibility

Overview

- What is strategic analysis?
- Analyze the external environment.
- Analyze the internal environment.
- Summarize in a SWOT matrix.

You have communicated top management's expectations, priorities, and deadlines to your team and got their buy-in. However, before you can start developing the short-term plans that underlie your budget, you need to analyze your internal and external operating environment. This will give your team a shared understanding of the opportunities that you can leverage, any threats you may face, the strengths of your team that you should capitalize on, and any weakness you must address.

What Is a Strategic Analysis?

A *strategic analysis* involves a thorough assessment of the external and internal environment of your organization. It should be conducted prior to the identification of goals and objectives and strategy formulation. It ensures that your team has a common understanding of the current state of the organization, its strengths and weaknesses, and which opportunities or threats need to be addressed in the future. Strategic analysis is the foundation for identifying the difference between where you are and where you want to be, which is also known as the *strategic gap*. Your *strategic plans* should strive to close this gap and bring the organization closer to its desired position over a reasonable period of time.

A *SWOT analysis* is commonly used to systematically assess an organization's operating environment. SWOT stands for strengths, weaknesses, opportunities, and threats. In the external environment, we identify opportunities and threats; in the internal environment we identify strengths and weaknesses. Tool 5-1 shows a list of possible external and internal factors that you should consider during your assessment of the operating environment. Your team should determine which factors are most relevant for your organization.

Tool 5-1

Factors to Consider in Your Strategic Analysis

External Factors	Internal Factors
Market	People
Industry	Business Processes
Technology	Information Systems
Economy	Policies and Procedures
Government	Financial Conditions
Society	Facilities

Analyze Your External Environment

How can you identify the major environmental forces that may affect your organization? One possible framework is the use of a *PESTLE analysis*—Political, Economic, Social, Technological, Legal, and Environmental. This analysis focuses on those external factors that are outside your organization's control, but will still have some level of impact. As you can see, the PESTLE framework is embedded in the external factors identified in Tool 5-1.

Your team should analyze the opportunities and threats in each major category as they pertain to your organization. While your team may identify several trends, they should only be included in the strategic analysis if they will have a major impact on your organization. Let us examine each external factor in more detail.

Market

The market analysis focuses on the customer. It seeks to identify the different market segments that you serve and the distribution channels you use to reach your customer. Some key questions to answer are:

- In what market segments do we operate? In what market segments should we operate?
- Are the market needs changing?
- Is the market growing, stagnant, or in decline?
- What is our current market share?
- Are we growing at, above, or below the market rate?
- What are our distribution channels?
- Are there new channels that we should be exploring?

Industry Structure

An understanding of your industry structure is critical for understanding the value proposition you offer to your customer and your competitive advantage. One popular framework for analyzing the industry structure is economist Michael Porter's *five forces* (Tool 5-2). According to Porter, the strength of these five forces will determine the level of competitiveness and the drivers of profitability in your industry.

Using the five forces analysis, spend time analyzing your competition and how you are positioned relative to your key competitors. What do they do extremely well? What are their weaknesses? What is your sustainable competitive advantage? What is their business strategy? Is their financial capability greater or less than yours? Is there a niche market that is unattended?

The Internet, market research companies, and other informal sources such as banking officers, suppliers, or your professional network can provide business intelligence on your competition. If your competitors are publicly held companies, you can find a significant amount of information on their website, including quarterly presentations to investors and quarterly and annual filings required by the Securities and Exchange Commission (SEC), which regulates these companies.

TOOL 5-2
A SUMMARY OF THE FIVE FORCES

Force	Definition
Threat of New Entrants	Identifies the difficulty in entering the industry. Barriers to entry could include technology, capital requirements, economies of scale, retaliation from existing competitors, and government regulation.
Bargaining Power of Buyers	Looks at the influence of your customers, such as the number of buyers, their ability to integrate backward, the buyer cost of switching to another product or company, and the impact of your business on buyer operations and costs.
Bargaining Power of Suppliers	Examines the influence of the suppliers, such as the number of vendors, the availability of substitute products, their ability to integrate forward, and the importance of your unit volume for their business.
Rivalry	Evaluates the competitiveness of the industry and examines market growth, product differentiation, number and diversity of competitors, industry capacity, and exit barriers, among others.
Threat of Substitutes	Examines the relative value of price and performance, buyer cost of switching, and buyer tendency to substitute.

The Internet, market research companies, and other informal sources such as banking officers, suppliers, or your professional network can provide business intelligence on your competition. If your competitors are publicly held companies, you can find a significant amount of information on their website, including quarterly presentations to investors and quarterly and annual filings required by the Securities and Exchange Commission (SEC), which regulates these companies.

Technology

Technological changes can have a deep and profound implication for your business. Think about how Amazon and eBay have upended the retail shopping experience or how driverless cars will change the way we live and work. Technological innovations can create new markets or destroy existing ones. It is extremely important to stay abreast of these changes in your industry. You do not want to be the next Polaroid (cameras) or Olivetti (typewriters), one-time market leaders in their industries who were displaced by digital technology.

Technological innovations not only affect the products and services that you provide but also your workplace. Think about the amazing changes you have experienced in your lifetime: the worldwide web, mobile devices, cloud computing, and videoconferencing, among many, many others. It is important that your team identify how technology will affect the products and services that you sell, as well as how you live and work.

STEP **5**

Economy

The events in a global economy can also have a major impact on your business. Analyze the economic outlook for the geographic regions in which you do business. Understand the key economic indicators—such as employment, GDP growth or decline, and consumer confidence—as well as how they may affect the demand for your products or services or your cost of doing business. Do you have any interdependencies? Does your business depend on the price of a critical commodity, such as oil, natural gas, or corn? These interdependencies should be clearly identified as part of your strategic analysis.

Government

Government policy and regulations can shake up and shape the commercial activities of any business. It is important to assess how changes in government regulations could affect your business, including new or proposed legislation that could require changes in your processes or increase your operating costs. Key areas to review should include labor laws, environmental regulations, health and safety regulations, labor laws, and taxes.

You should also evaluate the fiscal stability and governance of the country in which you operate. What is the government's fiscal condition? Is it sound or is it in deficit spending? Is there an impending threat of a repeal of tax incentives or an increase in the tax rate? How stable is the government? Will there be major policy changes if one party or another wins? How will this change affect your company?

Society

Finally, your team must evaluate the changing demographics and societal trends that may affect the demand for your products and how you manage the workplace. Some factors to consider include the composition of the labor force, educational opportunities, cross-cultural communication, and even religion! For example, rising longevity in the workplace has created new challenges, but also opened up new opportunities. In the last 20 years, diversity programs have become commonplace, as have policies and programs that support sustainability and social responsibility. The ability to foresee these demographic and societal changes will prevent your team from being blindsided by a trend for which you are unprepared to respond.

Analyze Your Internal Environment

Once you have analyzed the external environment, it is time to look inside your organization. An analysis of the internal environment will force your team to examine the strengths and weakness of your areas of responsibility, and allow them to assess how well the company is positioned to capitalize on the opportunities and manage the threats posed by the external environment. Six critical areas should be examined: people, business processes, facilities, information systems, policies and procedures, and the financial condition of the company.

People

As you examine the organizational structure and look at how you can be more effective (what you need to do to achieve better results) or efficient (how to do more with less), some areas to consider are the core competencies of your employees, compensation, organizational structure, absenteeism, turnover, and morale.

Business Processes

An analysis of your internal environment should include an evaluation of your key processes and activities. Key processes are those activities that add value to the customer or are critical to your organization's day-to-day operations, such as procurement, logistics, sales, customer service, technical support, production, quality control, and distribution. You should also examine how well your processes are being executed and whether there are any bottlenecks that need to be addressed. Talk to your customers, whether internal or external, and get their feedback. How do they evaluate your performance? What areas do you need to improve?

Facilities

Facilities relate to the physical conditions of your workplace. Your team should discuss the adequacy of your facilities and equipment to support current and future operations and if they comply with current government regulations. Other key issues involve safety, security, and business continuity. Do you have a documented business continuity plan in place—could you continue operations in the face of an unforeseen event or natural disaster?

Information Systems

Your team should examine the adequacy and robustness of your information technology (IT) platforms and systems support. Do you have an integrated system or are there islands of automation? Do you rely on in-house resources or external contractors to keep your systems running? Are your software applications updated regularly with new releases? Incredible as it may seem, we once had a client who had not updated their ERP system in 15 years!

Because communications are now integrated with computer applications, information systems should be analyzed in the broadest sense. Your analysis should also include telecommunications, such as the Internet, intranet, videoconferencing, and mobile devices, including data security and backup.

Policies and Procedures

Your team should also evaluate the policies and procedures of your organization and your areas of responsibility. Are all critical procedures clearly documented? Are they being followed? Do you have the right policies in place to motivate the desired behavior? The cases of Wells Fargo's fake account scandal and unwanted auto insurance policies are examples of how policies and procedures can motivate undesirable and even unethical behavior. Other areas to examine should include how frequently procedures are updated and the adequacy of the internal controls in your area. In addition, based on your analysis of the external environment, you may find that you need to create a new policy or procedure to address a specific legal or regulatory requirement.

Financial Condition

You should have a general understanding of the financial condition of your company. This understanding will help you establish your own financial ceiling on the amounts that you are requesting in the budget for your department. If you are a publicly held company, financial information will be available on your company website. If you are a privately held company, you may find it more difficult to obtain this information. Some privately held companies are very open about their financials and others hold it close to the vest. If your company is privately held and not forthcoming with its financial information, watch for key signals that may indicate that the company is doing well or poorly. Is there a problem with the collection of receivables? Has the company extended its payment terms to vendors? Is the company investing in capital equipment and employee training? These situations can be indicators of your company's financial condition.

Summarize in a SWOT Matrix

Once you have finished the assessment of your internal and external environment, you are ready to summarize the information to facilitate its use in developing strategies and action plans that we will discuss in step 6. You will have a lot of information, which needs to be digested and processed before you start the strategy formulation process. How do you focus the attention on the key issues that must be addressed in the next budgeting cycle? We recommend the following steps to help your team synthesize the critical issues that should be addressed in your strategic plan:

- Have your team go back over each category in the internal and external environments and agree on three to five items that will be a priority for the next planning cycle.
- Summarize the top items in a SWOT matrix, which will give you a quick overview of the issues that must be addressed over the next planning cycle.
- Keep your SWOT analysis summary as short and concise as possible. We encourage you to limit it to two pages.

Example 5-1 shows a sample one-page SWOT matrix for an online training company.

The Next Step

The strategic analysis is one of the most important steps of the planning process. It will take time and effort to do it properly, particularly if your team has never been involved in this type of exercise. However, the benefits that you obtain will more than compensate for the time and effort you invest in this process.

Beware of discussing possible solutions as you identify the issues your team needs to address. This situation is very common in these types of sessions and will probably require an experienced facilitator, who can keep the group focused and on track. Create a parking lot to place any possible issues and solutions that you do not want to discuss the moment they come up. This practice will ensure that they are not forgotten as you wrap up the process.

In summary, strategic analysis provides a shared understanding of the operating environment over the next planning cycle and allows your team to identify the major opportunities and threats in the external environment, as well as their readiness to address them by analyzing your strengths and weaknesses. Tool 5-3 includes a list of questions grouped by major category that can help guide your discussions as you commence this process. This analysis is the underlying foundation of the strategic formulation process, which we will discuss in step 6.

EXAMPLE 5-1

A SAMPLE SWOT MATRIX FOR AN ONLINE TRAINING COMPANY

Opportunities	Threats
• Increased use of mobile devices. • Investment in training is currently on an upswing. • Online learning provides an opportunity to reduce costs. • Users are demanding more flexibility as to how, when, and where they train. • Individuals perceive online learning as an alternative to live training. • VC firms are investing large sums in online education startups.	• Online training has a high drop-off rate, estimated at 91 to 93 percent for massive open online courses. • Corporate market is a slow adopter of newer technologies; 47 percent of training is still instructor-led. • Corporate market is more complex and has higher vendor requirements than the individual market. • Limited availability in the labor market in instructional design and development.
Strengths	**Weaknesses**
• Proprietary intellectual property. • Proven effectiveness in the corporate market. • Product fills a market void for continuing education in a specialized area. • Highly experienced multigenerational team. • Significant expertise in instructional design, delivery, and assessment of online educational programs. • Expertise in production and video editing skills. • Top-notch software developers.	• Website does not promote a sense of community. • Training modules have limited user interactivity. • Limited financial resources to grow the business. • Lack of sales and marketing expertise.

TOOL 5-3
KEY QUESTIONS TO ASK WHEN ANALYZING YOUR ENVIRONMENT

External Environment

Market

- What is our customer demographic? Are their needs being addressed by our products and services?
- Is there an unattended market need?
- What trends can we identify in the market that may affect the organization?
- What are the projected growth rates of the market segments in which we operate? Is there a market segment that we should enter?
- What is our current market share by geographic region? Are we growing at, above, or below the market rate?
- How do we distribute our products? Are there new channels that are worth exploring?

Industry Structure

- What is our sustainable competitive advantage?
- Who are our competitors?
- What do they do extremely well? What are their weaknesses?
- What is their business strategy?
- What is their financial capability? Is it more or less than ours?
- Is there a niche market that is unattended?

Technology

- What changes in technology can we foresee for the next three to five years?
- Are there any new technologies under development that may influence the demand for our product and services?
- Can we identify new or developing technologies that may affect the way we live and work?

Economy

- What is the economic outlook on a local, regional, national, or international level?
- What key economic indicators may affect our business?

- Where are our interdependencies?
- Does our business depend on a critical commodity, such as oil or natural gas?

Government

- What are the key regulatory agencies in each country where we do business?
- Is there any new or proposed legislation that could significantly affect us?
- Are there any changes in government policy that could affect the way we do business or increase our costs?
- Are there any international trade agreements under discussion? Are there any disputes?
- What is the government's fiscal condition? Is it fiscally sound or is it bankrupt?
- What is ease of obtaining business permits?

Society

- What are the demographics of the regions in which we do business?
- How have they changed over the last five years?
- What are the population trends and how will they affect us?
- Will demographic changes open up new markets?
- What changes in societal values or beliefs could affect how we do business or the types of products and services we offer in the future?

Internal Environment

People

- Is the organization structured correctly? Does it respond to the business needs?
- Can we restructure to increase the efficiency or effectiveness of our operations?
- Does our organizational culture facilitate or obstruct the achievement of our objectives?
- Do our employees have the right competencies? If not, how can they acquire these skills?
- Are we recruiting the right people? How long is the recruiting process by key position?
- Are our employees properly trained?

- Do they have opportunities for growth within the organization? Are there formal development opportunities for high-potential employees?
- Do we operate in a competitive labor market? Is our compensation package competitive relative to the market?
- What are employee turnover and absenteeism rates? Are we working a significant amount of overtime?
- What is the level of employee satisfaction?

Business Processes

- What are the major processes performed in our business unit?
- How well are these processes being executed?
- Is there a bottleneck? What is the root cause?
- What areas should we target for improvement that will yield the most benefits for the organization?

Facilities

- Are the facilities adequate for our current level of operations?
- What is our capacity utilization? Is it necessary to expand or shut down work areas or relocate facilities?
- Does the organization have written safety protocols? Are they being followed?
- Are the facilities adequately protected from unauthorized access? Is there a problem with theft on the premises?
- Do the facilities comply with government regulations? What areas are in noncompliance?
- Do we have a business continuity plan? How will we respond in the face of an unforeseen natural disaster or disruption to our operations?

Information Systems

- Does our current systems platform adequately support the business?
- Is there new technology that could improve the accessibility of information or provide a competitive advantage for the customer?
- Are our software applications updated regularly?
- Are we running key business applications on non-robust platforms?

- Do we have adequate information systems support? Is it internal or subcontracted? Do we have the necessary systems support for every shift?
- Do we back up our system on a regular basis? How often do we test the backup to ensure it works properly?
- Are systems processes and procedures documented?
- Do we have the most current security protocols in place?

Policies and Procedures

- Is there a manual that documents our key policies and procedures? Who updates this manual and how often? How are updates communicated?
- Do our policies motivate the desired behavior in our employees?
- Do we have procedures that are obsolete or hinder our ability to get things done?
- Do we have procedures that can be simplified?
- Do we have proper controls to safeguard company assets, including information?
- Do we need to revise or create new policies to support changes in the external environment?

Step 6

Develop Short-Term Objectives, Strategies, and Tactical Plans

Overview

- Define short-term objectives and key initiatives first.
- Develop strategies and action plans.
- Agree on key objectives for your areas of responsibility.
- Define performance measures.

By now, you should have a strong understanding of your company's long-term objectives, and the external and internal factors of the operating environment that you must address in your plan. You also should know where you need to focus your efforts to move the organization toward its desired future state. The next step is to define specific, short-term objectives and action plans for the budget horizon. These plans will determine the resource requirements that you will quantify into a budget for the next fiscal year.

Define Short-Term Objectives and Key Initiatives First

Short-term objectives are expected results that can be achieved within a short period of time, generally one year or less. Some objectives may take longer, depending on the complexity of the change desired.

Short-term objectives must be aligned with the overall company direction and their attainment should move you closer to the desired future state of the organization. Your objectives should leverage those strengths identified in the SWOT analysis and address any weaknesses. They should also seek to capitalize on any significant opportunities and attend to potential threats.

Key initiatives are specific projects that will move the organization to achieve its short-term objectives and should be included in your action plan. These initiatives should address one or more major issues identified in your SWOT analysis. You probably will not be able to tackle every issue identified during the budget year, so you will need to pick and choose which issues to address based on organizational priorities. Select those initiatives that will result in the big wins first and give you the biggest bang for your buck. Remember, employees still have to complete their day-to-day activities while engaged in the design and implementation of any key initiatives. Keep your key initiatives at a manageable level!

Develop Strategies and Action Plans

Recall from step 2 that strategies are mid- to long-term plans defined for a specific period, usually two to five years. They should support the company's mission, vision, goals, and objectives. Strategies describe how the company will achieve its long-term goals. They provide managers with a logical framework around which to organize and prioritize their detailed work plan. This plan will become the basis for the assignment of resources during the budget process.

You should limit the number of strategies. As a general rule, five to 10 strategies are more than enough, depending on the size and complexity of your organization. If your list of strategies is too long, it may be an indication that you have confused strategies with action plans. A long list may also overwhelm the organization and limit your team's ability team to execute.

Action plans, also known as *tactical plans,* outline specific initiatives, activities, programs, or tasks that you undertake to achieve your objectives. Remember, strategies are general in nature, whereas action plans detail exactly what will get done under each strategy, who will do it, and *when* it will be completed.

For example, suppose your company has a strategy to grow sales in Latin America. While there are many actions you can take to support this strategy, you specifically name three: identify suitable products, recruit and train bilingual employees, and open an office in Panama (Example 6-1).

EXAMPLE 6-1
SAMPLE STRATEGY AND ACTION PLAN

Strategy: Increase sales by growing the Latin American market.

Action Plan:
- Identify products that are suitable for the new market.
- Hire and train bilingual employees.
- Fund and staff a South American regional office in Panama.

STEP 6

Other managers or department heads, such as those in human resources or marketing, may also have a detailed action plans to support the strategy. During the budgeting process, it is important to identify key interdependencies and establish regular checkpoints with other areas from whom you will require support. This process will ensure these areas have assigned the right level of resources to support your work plan, resolve any potential conflicts, and avoid redundancy of efforts among the different departments.

Agree on Key Objectives for Your Areas of Responsibility

In step 2, we defined an objective as something specific the organization wants to accomplish. It represents a target or an expected outcome as a result of the actions outlined in your work plan during the budget period. Recall that your objectives should be *SMART:* specific, measurable, attainable, realistic, and time-bound.

You should discuss and agree on the short-term objectives for your areas of responsibility with your team based on your SWOT analysis and the expectations of senior management. These objectives can be quantitative or qualitative. *Quantitative objectives* are those that can be measured and tracked, and are generally understood in terms of numbers. They can be expressed in units per time period, per person, or some other measure of resource usage. Other examples include measures such as reducing set-up times by X percent, making a certain number of customer calls, or completing a specific output in a given time period.

Qualitative objectives, on the other hand, are more subjective and harder to measure. Because they reflect an opinion or point of view, the evaluation of the final outcome may differ based on the eye of the beholder. Objectives such as "improve customer satisfaction" may need to be measured either through customer surveys or by gathering information on the key dimensions that define a satisfied customer. For example, if your objective is to reduce the wait time for a service, you will have to make an assumption as to what your customer considers "acceptable." In establishing this target, you may need to identify how much improvement would be required before the customer's perception changes.

As you can see, multiple combinations of qualitative and quantitative objectives can be defined and tracked. When you select these measures, beware! There is an old saying, "you are what you measure." Your short-term objectives will significantly influence how your managers and employees behave and respond to different situations, particularly if you tie these to their annual salary increases and bonuses. We have seen may dysfunctional behaviors occur in organizations, resulting in millions of dollars of wasted resources, simply because managers had to complete an objective to receive their full bonus. Therefore, when setting specific goals or metrics, you must take care they are reasonable, doable, and verifiable. Managers and supervisors must be vigilant of any anomalies that signal a misuse or misunderstanding of any activities being measured. Now let's put this together using an example to show how you can set objectives, strategies, and action plans for your area.

Wells Fargo: A Case of Misused Metrics

Between 2011 and 2016, more than 5,000 Wells Fargo bank employees were asked to resign after it was discovered that they had created thousands of new accounts on behalf of existing customers without their consent. It was determined that a program rewarding employees for reaching certain goals (new products sold or accounts opened) resulted in the unintended consequence of encouraging employees to create new accounts by shifting funds between customer accounts so they could reap large bonuses for goals achieved. Once uncovered, the practice created a public relations nightmare for Well Fargo, which incurred significant fines and also had to return millions to their customers (Forbes 2016).

Suppose top management has communicated a market expectation that you will grow sales at a higher rate than the industry average over the next five years. An objective could be to "Obtain a 20 percent increase in sales revenue by the end of fiscal year 20XX." Now, assuming your industry is still growing, your products are still in demand, and you can compete successfully, you'll need to ask yourself the following questions:

- Is this objective **specific?** Yes; your goal is to increase sales revenue by 20 percent.
- Is it **measurable?** Yes; your company regularly tracks and reports revenue as part of monthly and quarterly operating reviews.
- Is it **attainable?** Well, that may depend on the actions you take, but since we have agreed that the industry is still solid and you can compete in the current market, we would venture to say yes!
- Is it **realistic?** If your plans are reasonable and can be achieved in the established timeframe, the answer would be yes!
- Is it **time bound?** Definitely; you have established an expected end date for fiscal year 20XX.

This objective, as defined, can be long term or short term. If year-end 20XX is more than two or three years away, it would be a long-term objective, in which case you may require short-term objectives in the interim years to ensure you are moving toward the end goal. If your industry is growing by leaps and bounds and you are expected to keep up or be left behind, you could set this as a short-term objective to be achieved within a one- to two-year timeframe. Now let's look at the whole picture again. Figure 6-1 shows the interrelationship of each element of the process.

FIGURE 6-1
THE INTERRELATIONSHIP OF THE ELEMENTS OF A PLAN

Our objective stated that we wanted to "Obtain a 20 percent increase in sales revenue by the end of fiscal year 20XX." Recall from Example 6-1 that "increase sales by growing the Latin American market" was the strategy identified to achieve this objective. By making this statement a strategy for the organization, you communicate that the company plans to enter the Latin American market. Any decisions made in the planning horizon should support this strategy. Note that it supports and aligns with the objective to increase total sales by 20 percent.

The next step is to develop specific action plans that allow the company to achieve that market penetration. Recall that action plans are specific initiatives, activities, programs, or tasks that are required for each strategy with the budget timeframe. Our strategy to increase sales is addressed by three specific action plans, one of which is to "identify products that are suitable for this new market." The sales and marketing manager would probably be responsible for developing the detailed work plan required to complete this item. Because the overarching goal is to increase sales in Latin America, they would be examining existing or new product offerings that could be sold in these markets as well as any information related to the sales activity. The manager would also have to determine what resources and interactions with other areas of the business they would require and establish a timeline for working through the details, including the budget needed to complete the plans.

Note that you may have as many objectives as you need to make sure you are moving toward the company's vision. However, as mentioned previously, make sure you don't overload the organization with a long list of objectives. Your ability to achieve the objectives will depend on the resources that top management is able and willing to commit.

The action plan completes the link from the company's vision, goals, objectives, and strategies to the specific activities that will take place during the next fiscal year to move the organization in the desired strategic direction. The budget will quantify the resources required to operationalize your action plan and achieve the expected business outcomes. Note that if these plans require additional resources beyond your normal operating budget, these incremental resources should be clearly identified as you put together your budget.

Top management should be careful not to overextend the available resources and to resolve any conflicting initiatives before the final budget is presented for approval. In step 8 we will discuss how to manage situations when budget constraints do not allow for the assignment of resources to every initiative presented as part of the final budget review. Remember, the ultimate objective of most organizations is profitability and sustainability. You must balance the continuation of your day-to-day business activities and the completion of the tasks listed in your action plan.

Define Key Performance Measures

Once you have developed your strategies and action plans, you must find a way to manage the progress of your organization. *Key performance measures,* also known as *key performance indicators* or *KPIs,* are quantifiable measures that an organization uses to evaluate and communicate progress toward objectives. Your organization probably has a set of key performance measures. You will need to determine if they are sufficient to allow you to track and monitor your plan or if you need additional measures. If additional metrics are required, you should define with your team what measures will be tracked, how the data will be collected, and the frequency with which they will be reported.

A word of caution: If possible, use existing metrics to measure your progress against the plan. Try to minimize manual data collection efforts that tie up precious resources in number crunching exercises while adding little value. Whenever possible, data should be collected automatically using existing information systems that provide timely, accurate, and verifiable figures. Technology has enabled the use of business intelligence systems that collect data and analyze in real time. A company with automated systems should be able to provide the necessary data to measure the progress toward your objectives. However, be aware that any system—whether a business intelligence system, an ERP system, or a spreadsheet application—will only be as good as the underlying configuration of the data and reports.

Let's return to our prior example of increasing sales revenue. You need to establish your goal for each metric and the expected completion dates. If your expectation is to increase sales by 20 percent in a four-year period, you need to determine a specific goal for each year. Should it be 5 percent per year, or is it more reasonable to set a goal of 2 percent the first year, 4 percent the second year, 6 percent the third year, and 8 percent the fourth year to reach the desired 20 percent? In any case, the goal should be agreed upon by the team responsible for carrying out the work and their manager. This goal setting can be a subtle negotiation, where a team's insight is weighted against top management's expectations; often, the stakeholders in the negotiation must reach a compromise, which takes into account the different points of view.

Once the objectives and metrics have been agreed upon, they will be included as part of the budget documentation to inform everyone in the organization of the commitments made and management expectations. This document will be the basis for progress review meetings, which will be held throughout the budget timeframe. Similar metrics can be established for each initiative or project so management can keep track of the status. The specific metric is designed based on the activities that need to be carried out and the relationship of the metric to the status or stage of completion.

Finally, don't forget to establish a regular review period. Although most organizations have a monthly management financial review, we recommend that you set aside a quarterly meeting to review the tactical plan's progress for each major functional area or business unit. In step 10, we will discuss a review process to ensure you are moving in the right direction.

The Next Step

At first glance, the development of short-term objectives, strategies, and action plans appears to be an overwhelming task that requires substantial amounts of time and effort. However, by involving key members of your team you can make it a less burdensome assignment. Their involvement should result in a better understanding of the tasks they are being asked to complete, more commitment to achieving established objectives, and a clear, documented road map for the next fiscal year. Make sure your objectives promote the desired behaviors in your organization.

A word of caution: Do not burden your managers and employees with so many objectives that they lose sight of the organization's main goal: to keep your customers happy and remain profitable.

Next, step 7 addresses how to prepare your departmental spending budget.

Step 7

Prepare Your Departmental Spending Budget

Overview

- Analyze the key activities of your department.
- Determine staffing requirements.
- Analyze your cost structure.
- Calculate major spending categories.

In step 6, you identified short-term objectives and developed detailed action plans. You are now ready to start working through the numbers to determine what resources you have, what resources you need, and whether your plans are financially aligned with the expectations of the organization.

The budget preparation process is the ideal moment for you to examine your departmental resources and how these are allocated among the activities performed by your department. It is the time to assess key business processes and determine if they can be done more efficiently in pursuit of organizational objectives. You will identify and agree on the key assumptions that underlie your budget calculations.

Analyze the Key Activities of Your Department

Every department has two types of activities: *primary activities,* which relate directly to the mission of your department or work area, and *secondary activities,* which support the primary activity. For example, in a production department, manufacturing the product is a primary activity, while data entry is secondary. In a call center, handing customer inquiries is a primary activity, while employee training is secondary. A general rule of thumb is that 80 percent of your resources should be dedicated to performing primary activities.

How do you analyze your department's key activities to determine opportunities for cost reduction or process improvement? Tool 7-1 includes a list of seven questions that you should ask to gain a better understanding of your activities and key processes. The questions provide a framework to analyze the activities of your department, find opportunities to improve your resource utilization, and identify non-value-added activities that could be eliminated.

TOOL 7-1
ANALYZING THE ACTIVITIES OF MY DEPARTMENT

1. What are the primary and secondary activities performed by my department?
2. What types of resources—people, equipment, or supplies—are required to perform these activities?
3. How much do these resources cost?
4. How are my resources distributed between primary and secondary activities?
5. What factors drive the costs of these activities? (For example, government regulations, customer requirements, and corporate policies.)
6. Are there inefficiencies or duplications with other areas that can be eliminated?
7. What specific actions can I take to lower costs in these activities without affecting quality or customer service? Are these included in my work plan?

Determine Staffing Requirements

As part of the departmental spending budget, you will probably be asked to submit a headcount plan. The *headcount plan* details the labor resources that you need to achieve your work plan for the upcoming year. Its preparation gives you a unique opportunity to ask hard questions about your organizational structure as you assess staffing requirements. How are your labor resources distributed by activity or key processes? Are your labor resources properly allocated to these key activities? If you had a blank slate and could start from scratch, would you organize the department differently? Do you have a problem employee who is affecting productivity and performance? Do you have the right skills in the right places? Is your organizational structure adequate for meeting the challenges of the future?

The preparation of the headcount plan is also a good time to consider alternate ways to structure your department. Can any activities be consolidated, centralized, or eliminated? Are tasks being performed that are unrelated to the primary mission of the department? Are you duplicating functions with another department?

After you have thoroughly examined your department, you are ready to determine your staffing requirements for the next budget period. The headcount plan should align with management expectations and support the work plan that you developed in step 6. Each organization has its own format for submitting this information, but it usually includes the job title of each position and, if currently filled, the name of the person who holds the position. If you are requesting new positions, you may be asked to provide a written justification as part of the budget documentation. Be sure to rationalize any requests for incremental headcount based your short-term objectives and work plan, which in turn should align with those of the organization. The ability to relate your headcount resources to specific mission critical activities and initiatives will facilitate the review process and your ability to communicate to the next level of management the impact of any budget cuts on your ability to execute your action plans.

STEP 7

The headcount plan receives a lot of attention during the budgeting process because it is the major driver of labor spending and other related expenses, such as training, travel, and employee relations. Be well-prepared to present and justify your headcount during the budget review process, which we will discuss in step 8.

Analyze Your Cost Structure

Before you start putting together your budget, you should have a thorough understanding of your department's cost structure. This understanding should be based on the departmental spending report you receive each month from the finance team, which compares actual to budgeted spending on a monthly and year-to-date basis. You have probably reviewed and explained the budget variances of this report many times. However, have you ever used it to examine the cost structure of your department?

Obtain a copy of your most recent departmental spending report. It should show the historical spending pattern for your department on a year-to-date basis, and may even have the forecasted spending levels for the current fiscal year. Also get a copy of the prior year's departmental spending report. Now examine the reports in detail. What are the most significant line items? Do you understand exactly what is being charged to each line item? Do you understand what should be charged to each line item? As you delve into the details, you may be surprised to find that items are being recorded in the wrong line, where you did not budget them, or that you are being charged for another department's or division's expenses. It is important to identify these errors and have them fixed by finance so that you have an accurate report of your departmental spending by line item.

Identify your recurring and nonrecurring expenses. *Recurring expenses* are incurred on a regular basis and can be estimated based on historical data. Examples include wages and salaries, overtime, utilities, rent, and depreciation. *Nonrecurring expenses* are incurred infrequently, primarily due to a special circumstance, such as a one-time event, a systems implementation, a new product introduction, or a government fine. Because of their infrequent nature, nonrecurring expenses should be isolated as you analyze your historical spending to ensure that you do not overestimate the line items in which they were recorded.

Of your recurring expenses, identify the variable, semivariable, and fixed costs. Variable costs are those that vary directly and proportionately with changes in sales or production volumes; some examples include production supplies, sales commissions, and direct labor. *Semivariable expenses* have a fixed and variable component; electricity and water are typical examples.

Fixed costs are those that do not vary with changes in volume, such as training, travel, and preventive maintenance. Most fixed costs in your department will be *discretionary costs,* which vary at the discretion of a manager. These costs are usually budgeted based on historical spending, capped by any restrictions placed by senior management and the general business environment. Travel and subcontractor expenses are particularly sensitive line items, so make sure you can justify the budgeted amount based on your short-term objectives and work plan.

Committed costs are fixed costs that result from contractual obligations, such as maintenance contracts or purchase agreements. They can also be a consequence of past decisions. For example, capital equipment purchases determine the depreciation expense that will be charged to your department. In general, committed costs cannot be altered in the short term, and represent fixed amounts that can be calculated very precisely.

A thorough understanding of your departmental cost structure will facilitate your preparation of budget estimates and help justify your spending levels during the budget review process. It also ensures that no significant expenses are overlooked. In the next section, we will discuss how to budget cost for the major expense categories in your department.

Agree on the Budget Assumptions

Before you start calculating the line items in your budget, you should agree with your team on the key assumptions that will underlie your calculations. Budget assumptions represent guidelines and expectations as to what will happen in the upcoming fiscal year. They determine your calculation of budgeted amounts and affect your ability to accurately estimate revenue and costs. Budget assumptions that cannot be substantiated with data or reasonable estimates will be challenged in a budget review. Your goal is to identify any budget assumptions that are reasonable and will hold up to scrutiny by the finance team and the next level of management.

Some assumptions are provided by the finance team when it issues the budget guidelines. These typically include assumptions that affect all departments, such as the rate of inflation, the estimated cost of key commodities (such as oil, gas, and precious metals), the cost of utilities, and salary increases. Finance may also provide guidelines on travel costs, employee activities, and employee training. You should always use their guidelines unless you have a pressing business reason to override them. If you choose not to use these guidelines, you must be prepared to build a strong business case to substantiate your need to use your own estimates.

In addition to the finance team's guidelines, you will need to identify any budget assumptions that are unique for your department. These assumptions would include the estimation bases for the cost of subcontracted services, equipment downtime, repair labor and parts, and overtime hours. Tool 7-2 lists the major spending categories in a typical departmental budget, the type of expenses that are budgeted in these categories, and possible estimation bases you could use to calculate the budget amount.

Tool 7-2

How to Estimate Your Departmental Spending

Spending Category	Type of Expense	Estimation Base
Salaries and Fringe Benefits	Base salary, payroll taxes, and other employee benefits	• Based on headcount plan • Usually calculated by the finance team
Overtime	Expected overtime costs for nonexempt employees	Number of overtime hours multiplied by the average labor rate per hour
Temporary Labor	Wages and salaries paid to temporary employees	Number of hours worked by temp employees multiplied by the average labor rate per hour
Maintenance	Maintenance labor and parts; may include maintenance contracts that pay a fixed charge each month, regardless of usage	• Agreed amount per vendor contract • Estimated hours multiplied by the average labor cost per hour • Parts based on historical usage and expected costs
Repairs	Repair labor and parts	Parts and labor based on historical usage and cost
Spare Parts and Tools	Miscellaneous tools, such as screwdrivers, nuts, and bolts	Based on historical costs (i.e., average costs per month)
Subcontracted Services	Outside contracted services, such as janitorial, security, and cafeteria	Based on contracted rates in service agreements
Operational Supplies	Production, cleaning, and safety supplies used in operations	Cost per employee or average cost per month
Office Supplies	Administrative supplies (e.g., paper, cartridges, and ink)	Average costs per month per employee

STEP 7

Spending Category	Type of Expense	Estimation Base
Expensed Equipment	All noncapitalized equipment (e.g., software, printers, tablets, and cartridges)	• Details of expected purchases and costs • Average cost per employee per year
Permits and Licenses	Permits and licenses required by government and regulatory agencies	Detailed listing of permits and licenses and their cost
Professional Service Fees	Payments made to lawyers, accountants, engineers, architects, and any other professional service; not to be confused with subcontracted services	• Estimated hours per service multiplied by the cost per hour • Contracted fee by month or year
Donations	Payments made to charitable organizations	• Based on historical spending or company guidelines • Can be budgeted in detail by organization or a lump sum amount

Calculate Major Spending Categories

Once you have determined the key assumptions, you are ready to start budgeting the different line items in your department. Not surprisingly, the largest departmental expense is labor. Additional expenses may include depreciation, utilities, travel, employee training, supplies, maintenance, and contractor fees.

Labor

Labor costs can represent more than 60 to 70 percent of your total departmental spending and are based on your headcount plan. Labor costs include salaries, payroll taxes, vacation and sick pay, commissions, bonuses, fringe benefits, overtime, and temporary employees. You probably will not be expected to calculate these line items for your department. In many organizations, the finance department will calculate labor spending for you, based on the information contained in the headcount plan. Because salaries are confidential and very sensitive, some organizations prefer not to provide their managers with detailed access to this information. Smaller organizations may require a manager to calculate the wages and salaries line in the budget based on the detailed salary information for each position in the headcount plan. Payroll taxes and fringe benefits are usually calculated by finance.

Budgeted labor costs should include projected salary increases. There are different ways to incorporate salary increases into the budget. Some companies establish a fixed percentage as part of the budgeting guidelines (for example, 2 percent of base salaries); during the year the manager will be expected to manage salary increases to that budgeted number. Other organizations require their managers to budget salary increases based on expected performance or some other basis, such as an increase in the minimum wage or union negotiations.

Depreciation

Depreciation is a method used by accountants to spread the cost of an asset over the number of periods it is expected to benefit the organization. Finance usually provides the budgeted depreciation expense based on your fixed assets listing, which contains detailed information on the assets you are accountable for that are assigned to your department. The budget depreciation amount should include the depreciation expense for all existing equipment and any new equipment that will be purchased in the upcoming year. The cost of any new equipment should also be included in the capital budget.

Do not take the budgeted depreciation figure provided by finance as a given. Make sure the amount provided is reasonable based on your knowledge of the department's existing equipment and any future purchases you included in the capital budget. Review the latest fixed asset listing for your area to ensure all assets in your department are properly accounted for and that you are not being charged for equipment that has been transferred, sold, or discarded. If you have not filled out the proper paperwork to notify the finance department, these assets will continue to accumulate depreciation costs, even though they are no longer physically in your department. If you believe the budgeted depreciation number is too high or too low based on your operational knowledge, work with your finance liaison and review how the numbers were calculated.

Other Expenses

Other expenses may include water, electricity, travel, training, supplies, maintenance, and subcontractor fees. There are several ways to estimate these types of expenses.

Use Historical Costs

Although historical costs may not be indicative of future spending levels, they can provide a solid basis for estimating expenses. If your department has spent an average of $2,000 in office supplies over the past two years, you could safely budget the same amount for the following year given no significant changes in business conditions. However, you can always modify estimates based on historical data to consider the impact of future events, such as price changes or new equipment purchases.

Obtain Vendor Quotes

Use this cost estimation method when historical data is unavailable or a price change is expected from a major vendor. Most vendors will gladly provide a quote for a product or service, which can be used to support your budgeted amount. Maintenance services, special events, and advertising campaigns are some examples of items that can be budgeted using vendor quotes.

Estimate Based on Expected Usage

Some costs can be directly related to resource consumption. You can calculate the budgeted amount by estimating the resource usage and multiplying it by its expected cost for the next fiscal year.

Suppose you are budgeting electricity costs for a production facility. Based on the budgeted production plan, you estimate the kilowatt usage at 100,000 kilowatt hours (kwh) per month. The cost per kilowatt hour is expected remain stable at $0.10. The budgeted electricity cost for the year would be $120,000 (100,000 kwh per month x 12 = 1,200,000 kwh x $0.10 per kwh = $120,000).

Be sure to identify the proper activity measure that describes how the resource is consumed. In the example, the activity measure is kilowatt hours. Other common activity measures include the number of employees, the units produced or sold, machine hours, labor hours, and cubic meters.

Use Comparable or Benchmark Data

Sometimes, it is possible to find publicly available data on the Internet that you can use to determine your estimates. Finding comparable or benchmark data is particularly helpful if you are starting a new project or program and have no historical data on which to project your operating expenses. Benchmark data provides a starting point for estimating your departmental spending. This data should be adjusted as necessary to reflect the reality of the local operating conditions. For example, ATD's *State of the Industry* report contains benchmark data that organizations in the training industry can use to estimate training costs. If you work in a large multinational company, you could gather comparable data from other sites that provide similar products or services to your own facility.

Benchmark data can also serve as a reality check to test the reasonableness of the budgeted amounts. If the budgeted figures are significantly higher or lower than similar operations in other parts of the organization or the industry standard, you must be prepared to explain this difference.

STEP 7

Document Assumptions, Risks, and Opportunities

We cannot emphasize enough the importance of documentation. Document everything! This documentation should include your key assumptions, sources of information, and any important conversations with team members, colleagues, or bosses that affected your budget calculations. People tend to have short memories, particularly if there is a large budget variance during the year. We recommend that you prepare a memo for file that documents any changes to a budgeted amount, including the name of the person who requested the change and the date and time of the discussion. You may never use it, but it may come in handy during the year.

You should also document any significant risks and opportunities if there is a reasonable chance that such a situation may surface during the next fiscal year. These risks may include an increase or decrease in the cost of key commodities, project delays, mergers and acquisitions of key suppliers, upcoming contract negotiations, or changes in government regulations. Note these situations in this section and, if possible, include an estimate of their potential financial impact. Your ability to foresee and document a situation as a possible risk or opportunity during the budget process will make it easier to explain a budget variance during the year.

The Next Step

Your departmental spending budget is the financial quantification of the resources you need to accomplish your short-term objectives and work plan for the next fiscal year. In this step, we discussed how to estimate the cost of these resources in a reasonable manner that will hold muster under management scrutiny. It is strongly recommended that you document your cost estimation methods for each significant line item in your budget. If the method is not documented properly, a challenge during the budget review process may deteriorate into a discussion of the estimation methodology, instead of the business issues underlying the numbers.

Pay particular attention to those line items that tend to draw a lot of management scrutiny, regardless of the budgeted amounts. These items typically include employee travel, overtime, temporary labor, subcontractors, and professional services. Senior management often considers these discretionary costs, which can be easily cut with no visible impact to the operations. Your ability to tie the quantification of your resource requirements to the primary activities of your department, its short-term objectives, and your detailed work plan will allow you to enter the budget review process from a position of strength and increase the probability of budget approval with minimal, if any, cuts.

Next, on to step 8, which examines the approval process and how to manage the different levels of review.

STEP **7**

Step 8

Obtain Approval for Your Budget

Overview

- Understand and manage the review process.
- Come to grips with budget cuts.
- Always have a plan B.

Review is a stressful and difficult part of the budgeting process. You will probably spend countless hours preparing presentations and attending meetings to present your plans to the next level of management. Hard questions will be asked, and discussions may get heated.

While we cannot guarantee that the review process will get easier after you read this step, it will give you a better understanding of how the process works and help you feel more prepared to defend your budget to outside scrutiny. As you navigate this process, never lose sight of the end goal: to obtain the necessary resources to execute your work plan, as quantified in the budget.

Understand the Review Process

The review process is the moment where you present your budgeted spending levels for approval. Obtaining the buy-in and approval of your boss is the first and, for you, probably the most important step in this process. However, recognize that as the budget moves through the organizational hierarchy, your numbers will be consolidated into larger organizational units, such as a manufacturing site, business unit, division, or a region, and will be subject to another level of analysis and negotiation. While the review with your manager may be very detailed, subsequent review levels will be more high level. Any revision requests will probably trickle down to you as a specific percentage or dollar amount that you must cut from your budget.

Consult With Finance

Before you present your budget for approval, have it reviewed by your financial analyst to ensure your numbers are credible. The financial analyst can verify that your numbers are accurate and reliable and point out inconsistencies between the budgeted amounts and the departmental goals or objectives. For example, we have reviewed budgets where a manager has new hires in the headcount plan but does not budget for their desks, chairs, or equipment.

Financial analysts ensure that all costs that should be included in your budget are accounted for. They can also help you identify inconsistencies or highlight unusual trends that may be questioned by the next level of management. For example, why are the actual figures higher or lower than the amounts proposed in the budget? Did you consider an alternate vendor for a significant expense item? Are your functions being duplicated in other departments? Are you performing functions that rightfully belong elsewhere? Finally, your financial analyst can check your budget submission to ensure that all required documentation has been properly completed and conforms to the expectations of the next level of management.

Share With Your Manager

Once your budget has been reviewed by the finance department, you are ready for the next step—the review with your manager. We hope that prior to this meeting, you have already met with your manager to discuss the priorities and expectations for the next fiscal year. The review process will involve the presentation of your work plan and the resources that you require to achieve it.

How much pushback you receive during this process will depend on your manager's leadership style. Some managers take a hands-off approach and, if the numbers seem reasonable, will not examine in great detail how you arrived at the budgeted amounts. Other managers take a more micro approach and will nitpick every line item in your budget, regardless of the dollar amount.

In general, your manager will prod, probe, and question your budget during the review process looking for inconsistencies or duplication of functions that result in an inefficient use of resources. Think of the management review as a negotiation process. You present what you need in monetary terms and negotiate these figures up or down (usually down) until you strike a reasonable compromise. If your manager believes that your budget will be unacceptable to the next level of management, you will be asked to rework the numbers.

Come to Grips With Budget Cuts

Budget cuts produce a high level of stress and frustration, particularly when they are arbitrary and spread evenly across the organization like peanut butter. The reviewing manager will often assume that you have padded your budget by hiding "fat" in obscure line items. As a result, you will probably be asked to cut your spending to meet the organization's financial targets. If you prepared your budget carefully, it will be almost impossible to do so without affecting your established plans for the budgeted year. Therefore, it is important that you bring your team together if you are asked to make budget cuts and discuss as a group how this reduction will be handled.

Reach Agreement With Your Team

You should avoid making arbitrary adjustments simply to comply with the required reductions. This decision will eventually come back to haunt you. Meet with your team and agree on the top priorities for your department, division, or business unit. Your goal should be to reach a consensus on which programs, projects, or line items to cut and by how much. What plans can be postponed until the next fiscal year? What plans should be eliminated altogether? What areas are critical to the organization? Can they continue to function effectively with the proposed budget cuts?

Managers, supervisors, and key employees involved in the budgeting process often complain bitterly that budgets are cut without their input or knowledge and without changing the performance expectations of their areas of responsibility. Holding a team meeting provides a forum to discuss the budget cuts as a group and understand the tradeoffs for your department or organizational unit as a whole. This could also reduce hard feelings toward the finance team, because they are merely the process facilitators, with your team in the driver's seat.

Prepare for More Review and Revision

The budget review and approval process will consist of one or more iterations and can take anywhere from one to two months. Senior management will continue to revise the budget until the financial results are in line with their expectations. While you may agree with your manager to make a series of cuts, once the budget is submitted to the next level for review you may be asked for additional cuts. In some organizations, the approval process gets so political and contentious that the fiscal year starts without an approved budget. This situation can create mayhem in the organization.

Once your budget has been approved, meet with your staff to go over the final budgeted amounts. This meeting will ensure that everyone is on the same page and is clear on what they are expected to accomplish with the approved resources.

Always Have a Plan B

Plan B consists of how your work plan will change depending on the budget reductions you are required to make. If you met with your team during the budget preparation process and established the priorities for your area, you probably have an idea of your plan B. If not, you will have to develop this plan as you come to grips with the required budget cuts.

We recommend that you evaluate three scenarios: a best case, a worst case, and a most likely case. The best-case scenario assumes your budget will be approved as submitted and you will get all the resources required to achieve your work plan for the next fiscal year. The worst case assumes a deep budget cut, which can severely affect your departmental operations. The most likely scenario assumes a manageable budget cut.

How do you determine the level of budget cuts under the most likely and worst-case scenarios? First, evaluate the financial condition of your company. Are revenues growing, stagnant, or in decline? Has there been a major catastrophic event, such as a product recall, a major lawsuit, a hurricane, an earthquake, or any other type of unforeseen situation that has increased operating costs? Is your company meeting shareholder expectations? The situational assessment that you performed as part of your strategic analysis in step 5 can provide clues as to what to expect during the budget review process. You should also look to past budgeting exercises. How much have you been asked to cut in prior years? Were the circumstances similar to the present or were they radically different? Armed with this information, you are ready to develop plan B with your team.

There is no rule of thumb or magical number we can give you to identify the percentage budget cut you should assume for your worst-case and most likely scenarios, other than to base it on your own experience and particular circumstances. For the worst-case scenario, we recommend that you identify the deepest budget cuts you have been required to make in the past three to five years, and then adjust that number based on your company's current financial situation. For the most likely scenario, you can assume a modest budget reduction, such as 5 percent, but again, your own track record will be the best guide.

As you develop your plan B, remember to avoid arbitrarily cutting dollars without understanding the implications for your organization. Get your team involved. Listen to their concerns about how budget cuts will affect their ability to execute the work plan or even jeopardize day-to-day operations. Remember, budgeting is not an exercise for the Lone Ranger.

Manage the Review Process

You can spend hours and hours preparing your budget, but this effort will get you nowhere if you do not learn to manage the review process. Tool 8-1 helps you navigate the process by summarizing the major dos and don'ts, which can be divided into two major categories: preparation and documentation.

Tool 8-1
Dos and Don'ts to Get Your Budget Approved

Do	Don't
• Know your manager's expectations. • Tie spending to your objectives, volume, or key initiatives. • Identify and quantify cost reductions. • Document your assumptions! • Prepare for the review. • Have a plan B.	• Take last year's budget and make minor adjustments. • Have a work plan that does not align with company expectations. • Make arbitrary cuts without communicating their impact. • Attend the review meeting unprepared.

Adapted from Oliver (2017).

Preparation

Make sure you understand your manager's expectations. For example, if the company asks for productivity improvements, be prepared to show how they are reflected in the budget. Know the level of detail your manager requires and the preferred presentation format.

It's also important that you do not overwhelm your manager with detailed or complex calculations. Keep it simple! If possible, summarize your work plan in a one-page document and tie it to your headcount and budgeted dollars. We know that sounds difficult to do, but

STEP 8

it can be done. It is also a very effective mechanism for presenting the big picture and avoiding getting mired in the details. Tool 8-2, which you'll find at the end of this step, provides an example of a one-page budget summary.

Documentation

Document everything! Sometimes numbers get changed hastily in the midst of a discussion or late at night without being properly documented. You may later find yourself scratching your head trying to figure out where a number came from. It has happened to us! If your manager tells you to make a change, make sure that you communicate and document the risks it may entail for the organization. This documentation will also be helpful if you need to explain budget variances that ensue later during the fiscal year.

The Next Step

The budget review process is the last—and possibly most important— step of the budgeting cycle. You must convince the next level of management that you have a well-thought-out plan for the next fiscal year; one that is aligned to organizational priorities and fiscally responsible.

In this step, we have described how to successfully navigate this process. Advance preparation and documentation are key factors that will allow you to defend your budget successfully and differentiate you from other managers in your organization who may enter the process ill-prepared.

A final word of advice: Do not provide more information than asked; it may open you up to further, unnecessary scrutiny. Remember that your goal is to obtain the necessary resources to execute your work plan. Hope for the best, prepare for the worst. The results may surprise you! We now move on to step 9, which takes you through the communication process after your budget has been approved.

STEP **8**

Tool 8-2

Sample Budget Summary

One-Page Budget Summary
Fiscal Year 20XX

Major Assumptions

Volume	Budget	Last Year	Inc/Dec	%
Sales or production volume (in units)	150,000	125,000	25,000	20.0
Service hours	10,750	9,800	950	9.6
Customer calls	12,000	10,000	2,000	20.0

You should select the operational measure used to calculate your revenues for the budget period and provide any significant explanation for the change. For example, the increase is a result of opening a new store or adding additional sales people.

Headcount	Budget	Last Year	Inc/Dec	%
Number of employees	12	10	+2	20.0

Generally, changes in headcount need to be justified, as in many companies; wages and salaries are one of the top spending categories. For example, we will be adding one salesperson and one warehouse employee to support volume increases.

Major Spending Categories

	Budget	Last Year	Inc/Dec	%
Salaries and wages	$350,000	$290,000	$60,000	20.6
Utilities	25,000	24,000	1,000	4.1
Materials expense	15,000	12,000	3,000	25.0

You should include major categories of spending and explain differences that are not obvious to the manager to whom you are presenting the data. Other data that could be presented include proposed salary increases or changes in employee benefits and expected material cost increases or inflation factors used.

STEP 8

Budgeted Capital Expenditures

Equipment purchases	$55,000
Increase in depreciation	$5,500
Equipment write-offs	$5,000
Decrease in depreciation	$200

Since the capital budget is often worked separately by the finance team, you should be able to explain the effect on your depreciation expense due to new equipment purchases or equipment being retired or disposed of.

Financial Performance Summary (Business Unit/Region)

	Budget	Last Year	Inc/Dec	%
Revenues or sales	$750,000	$590,000	$160,000	27.1
Cost of sales	487,000	389,000	98,000	25.2
Period expenses	90,000	65,000	25,000	38.5
Net income	$173,000	$136,000	$37,00	27.2

If the presentation is made at the business unit or regional level, you may have to provide a financial performance summary, which shows the impact of the proposed budgets on the net income or bottom line.

This section should include mention of any risk factors that could affect the outcome of the proposed plans, such as if you expect to renegotiate pricing on certain materials, or if you are counting on a specific contract to be signed by a certain date, or the successful installation of new equipment. These factors will give the reviewing manager some assurance that you have covered all the bases.

STEP
8

Step 9

Communicate Plans and Priority Projects

Overview

- Explain the approved budget to your team.
- Communicate plans and priority projects.
- Explain key initiatives.
- Explain any major budget cuts.
- Communicate management expectations.
- Document your discussions.

You have survived the review process and your budget has been approved. You have made all the required changes and updated your documentation. Now it is time to meet with your team members and communicate what was approved, the priority projects, and the effects of any budget cuts on the plans for the next fiscal year. This process of cascading down the finalized plan and budgeted dollars will be the same whether you are responsible for only one department or an entire organization. You must clearly communicate the end result of the budget process and management expectations to everyone in your department, and in particular to those who helped you put together the numbers.

STEP 9

Explain the Approved Budget to Your Team

When you assemble your team to discuss the budget, you should begin by identifying any challenges and areas of concern. You will review the assumptions used and request feedback from your team. This discussion is not meant to revisit or revise the assumptions, but to make sure your team is aware of how the assumptions were used and the impact on the final budget. You should air specific concerns by individual team members and clear up your expectations. As the manager accountable for the execution of the plans submitted and approved, you need to make sure that all members of your team fully understand their roles and responsibilities in achieving the desired results.

If your budget was not approved as submitted, you should discuss with your team how your action plans need to change based on resource constraints and assess your ability to meet the established objectives. Can your team meet the performance objectives without sacrificing compliance, quality, or customer service? Will the organization be placed at risk? In this meeting, the team can raise red flags to discuss with the next level of management. You should document and convey to management any perceived risks and what your plans are to reduce or eliminate them within the constraints of the approved budget.

Communicate Plans and Priority Projects

During the development of your work plan, your team identified major business objectives, including key projects and initiatives for the budget horizon. Now it is time to review this work plan and see if you need to reshuffle your resources in light of the approved budget. This discussion should highlight those projects and initiatives that are high priority for the next fiscal year.

Your staff should be clear on whether they are the driver of a project or are expected to provide a supporting role. They should understand that whenever they have to decide between conflicting activities, they should consider the impact on any major objective of your department or business unit. It also means that they may have to prioritize among conflicting activities. Make sure that they keep you, the manager, apprised of their prioritization scheme, because you may want to discuss their priorities given the needs of the organization as the year unfolds. This initial discussion will ensure that your team marches to the beat of the same drum with clearly established priorities.

A common concern of lower-level employees when faced with additional tasks or projects is how to manage the day-to-day operations and still meet project due dates. At times, they may feel overwhelmed while trying to do both. In this meeting, you may want to establish a clearly defined communication process within your department to manage these conflicts and resolve them in a timely manner. Any escalation process should include an open line of communication with all managers involved and the identification of an acceptable resolution for all parties. Any agreement should be documented adequately to avoid misunderstandings in the future.

STEP **9**

Explain Key Initiatives

The next step is to discuss in detail those initiatives that were assigned to your specific work area (or organization). As each initiative is discussed, you should identify the team member or manager who will serve as the main contact for any decision making that would affect the progress of the activities being worked on. In our experience, the assignment of resources to a given project is a common source of conflict among team members. Even when additional resources are approved to work on a new initiative, more experienced employees will get assigned to the project while the replacements are used in the day-to-day activities. However, if no new resources are approved, the burden of the additional work may still fall on your most experienced employees. You should expect some pushback from these employees and be prepared to listen and offer alternatives to lessen the impact on their workload. In some cases, you may need to make changes in your department to address any uneven workload created by the proposed plan.

If new resources are approved, now is the time to plan for how to recruit these additional resources. What was approved? Was it full-time employees or subcontracted services? If new hires were approved, are they available internally or will you have to recruit outside the organization? The amount of time you devote to this activity will depend on the number of new hires or the amount of the contract, the available labor or vendor pool to provide the services, and the level of specialized knowledge that may be required to complete these tasks.

Plan for a two- to six-month recruiting window if you are hiring new employees. This timeframe spans from the moment you post the job to the date the employee shows up to work in your area. This time horizon may vary according to the available labor pool in your area and whether the job requires specialized knowledge, which may lengthen the recruitment process.

Explain Any Major Budget Cuts

Management will rarely give you more resources than requested in your original budget submission. If they performed major surgery on your final approved budget, you probably did not get the resources you requested and will need to rethink your work plan in light of the reduced funding. You should have already thought this through with your team in step 8 when you were creating your plan B, but now is the time to put that plan into action.

First, you should explain the nature of your team's budget cuts and why they were made. Maybe it was because spending levels in general were too high and management issued across-the-board cuts to all business units to meet shareholders' expectations. There may also be very specific reasons for budget cuts, such as lack of alignment with strategic objectives or low priority for top management. It is important that you explain these reasons to your team, assuming that they were explained to you, to avoid increased frustration and decreased morale. Your team worked very hard to put the work plan and the budget together. They deserve a reasonable explanation as to why the budget was cut.

Second, listen to and acknowledge their concerns. In many cases, you will get a lot of pushback from those employees or areas affected by the cuts. Address them with action plans that are credible and doable. As a team, determine how the approved resources will be allocated, which projects are critical, and which can be postponed or eliminated.

Third, avoid getting drawn into a grievance session. Do not allow team members to get on their soap box of why they simply cannot live with the funds assigned. Be positive and have them present alternatives of what could be done within the budget constraints. Once the budget is approved, you and your team will be held accountable for its execution. As a team, you need to figure out how this will be done!

STEP **9**

Communicate Management Expectations

Managing a budget means making sure the tasks get done on time and spending no more than was assigned to carry out such tasks. Keeping within a budgeted time and dollar goal is a bit more complicated than you would think. You need to understand how the next level of management will hold you and your team accountable for the budget. Will it be the total for the department or will they be looking at individual line items? A budget will be easier to manage if you can compensate for overspending in one line with underspending in another.

You will also have to determine timelines for obtaining the necessary resources, which will often require relying on others to make sure progress is on track. Stoplight and variance analysis, which are explained in step 10, are two tools you can use to track progress against objectives and monitor actual spending levels against the approved budget.

You must be clear about reporting deadlines and information requirements established by management to examine actual results against the budget. A more detailed discussion of this management review process is presented in step 10.

Document Your Discussions

By the time you finish meeting with your team, they should have a clear understanding of management expectations, the resources available, and any issues surrounding the approved budget. Remember to prepare the minutes of this meeting, along with copies of any nonconfidential information presented, and distribute this document in a timely manner to the members of your team. The minutes should reflect any agreements made, any changes to the expected timing of tasks, and any concerns raised during the meeting. It should be kept as part of your annual budget review package because it will help resolve any questions or issues that may arise in the future. Tool 9-1 presents a sample of items and topics that should be covered in the minutes.

TOOL 9-1

PREPARING THE MINUTES OF YOUR BUDGET MEETINGS

There is no set format for preparing the minutes of your budget meeting. However, as we have stressed throughout this book, it's important to properly document your processes and decisions for future reference and conflict resolution.

The length and amount of detail contained in the minutes will depend on the complexity of the organization, the project, and even size of the team assigned. Keep the minutes as short and concise as possible! In addition, there should be a person responsible for preparing and publishing the minutes, which should be sent out no later than 48 hours after the meeting. Any corrections, revisions, or comments should be referred to the preparer for review. If the minutes contain a significant error, they should be reissued to all meeting attendees.

Below is a sample of the type of information that should be included in the minutes.

Meeting Date	Enter the date when the meeting was held. Include the month, day, and year.
Location	Where was this meeting held? On your premises, off-site, or in another facility?
List of Attendees	First and last names of everyone who attended the meeting.
Absent	First and last names of anyone who missed the meeting. Copy their manager.
Excused	First and last names of anyone who had a valid personal or business reason to miss the meeting.
Items Discussed	What agenda items were covered during the meeting? If an agenda item was not covered, or the discussion of the item was postponed, it should be noted in the minutes. If an item was covered that was not part of the original agenda, it should also be noted.

STEP 9

Decisions Made	Below each topic of discussion, document any important decision that was made. Any decision should identify who is responsible for its implementation and the expected timeframe for completion. In addition, you should document how these decisions will be communicated to the key players in your organization, and whether you need the approval from the next level of management.
Action Item Pending	Document which action items are pending and if they are on track or have been delayed. Note any problems and how they are being addressed.
New Issues	What new issues surfaced during the meeting? Were they discussed or was the discussion tabled for the next meeting? Are there any surprises that could affect the budget timetable?
Action Items for Next Meeting	What action items need to be addressed or completed by the next meeting? Any items should identify the person responsible and the due date, particularly if a document needs to be circulated prior to the meeting for review by the meeting attendees.
Parking Lot	Any issues that could not be resolved, require further study, or are not urgent are often listed separately and put in a "parking lot." This list ensures that important issues that were tabled for future discussion are not forgotten.

The Next Step

This step highlighted the importance of communication. The time spent with your team reviewing the final outcome of the budget process will be well worth it. Your team will feel more empowered and committed, and you will avoid pushback that often results from issues that were never discussed. Step 10 completes the planning cycle—you plan, budget, execute, review your performance against the plan, and then prepare to act.

Step 10

Review Performance Against Plan and Act!

Overview

- What is a budget variance?
- Analyze your performance against the budget.
- What next? You must take action!
- Understand the importance of a financial forecast.

You have completed the budget exercise; all your ducks seem to be lined up in a row. Your team members and any responsible managers have been adequately informed and have agreed on the budget numbers, corporate objectives, and performance measures to be used in the upcoming year. Now it is time to perform. Each group will be working on their assigned tasks and collecting data to report on their performance. You, as a manager, have the responsibility to stay informed of the progress being made and should provide your team with a forum to discuss and, if necessary, revise the direction, timing, or execution of specific tasks detailed in your work plan based on changes in the operating environment.

STEP **10**

What Is a Budget Variance?

It's wishful thinking that you can always meet your budget estimates, be it sales or spending amounts. More likely than not, your actual spending on any one budget item will not equal the amount you estimated and included in your approved budget. These differences are called budget variances and are classified as favorable or unfavorable. A favorable variance can occur when you spent less than what you budgeted or earned more revenue than you planned. Likewise, if you spent more or earned less than planned, you will incur unfavorable variances. At a very high level, when talking about total sales revenue or net earnings, an unfavorable variance is also known as a miss, while favorable variances are called beats.

Analyze Your Performance Against the Budget

One of a manager's most feared tasks is having to explain to a boss why more was spent than budgeted. Perhaps this is why the review step is often overlooked. Companies can get into major financial problems if they do not analyze budget variances in a diligent or timely manner. As a result, the impact of a budget variance on the future financial performance of the organization is not always discussed or well understood.

Spending: Actual Versus Budget

During the budget preparation process, you made assumptions about the operating environment and estimated the resources required to achieve the company objectives. As you move from planning to execution, these assumptions will be validated through budget reviews and the use of performance measures to evaluate your progress. As time goes by and tasks are carried out, money spent and recorded on the company's books will provide a financial picture of your business and how you are performing against expectations.

An analysis of your actual to budgeted spending levels deals mainly with money spent during the period to be reviewed. Typically, the finance team will provide a departmental budget report each month showing actual to budgeted spending for the month and year to date; it may even forecast performance for the year. You must also examine other performance measures, which may be financial, because they will help reveal your progress against stated objectives. Remember that the budget measures efficiency, not effectiveness. You may be right on target with the budget, even if you have not achieved any of your stated objectives for the fiscal year.

The financial review can be carried out at various levels in the organization. Depending on the audience and the size of the organization, these reviews may involve only top management, or they may involve middle management and project owners. The process is often the same, only the specific budget items reviewed will change. At the top management level, the financial review will probably be done at a financial statement level. Example 10-1 shows a pro forma income statement that can be used for discussion purposes. This statement presents a summary of revenues and expenses and compares actuals for an entire year with the budget for the same period.

EXAMPLE 10-1
SAMPLE INCOME STATEMENT

XYZ Corporation
Pro Forma Income Statement

	Year 20XX Actuals	% Net Sales	Year 20XX Budget	% Net Sales	Variance Over (Under)	% Variance
Net Sales	$2,600,000	100	$2,000,000	100	$600,000	30
Cost of Sales	950,000	37	800,000	40	150,000	19
Gross Margin	1,650,000	63	1,200,000	60	450,000	38
Operating Expenses						
Selling	156,000	6	120,000	6	36,000	30
Marketing	182,000	7	120,000	6	62,000	52
Research and Development	182,000	7	100,000	5	82,000	82
Administrative	300,000	12	200,000	10	100,000	50
Total Operating Expenses	820,000	32	540,000	27	280,000	52
Net Income	$830,000	32	$660,000	33	$170,000	25

STEP 10

Top management generally focuses on the "top line," meaning sales or revenue, and the "bottom line," referring to net income or EBIT (earnings before interest and taxes). These line items are watched closely by owners, directors, shareholders, and the investment community at large to gauge if a company will meet the expectations agreed upon and communicated at the end of the budgeting process.

There are two ways you can analyze your financial reports to gain insights into your performance against the budget. A vertical analysis shows the relationship of the income statement components against an established base, usually net sales. For example, when you prepare your budget you should compare sales to cost of sales with other companies in a similar industry using a ratio called the *gross margin percentage*. Gross margin is the difference between *net sales* and *cost of sales*. It is the amount left over after recovering the cost of the products sold to cover operating expenses, such as sales and marketing, distribution, administration, and research and development.

The *gross margin percentage* is a performance measure that shows gross margin as a percentage of net sales. Example 10-1 shows a healthy gross margin percentage of 60 percent, which is more than enough to cover all other operating expenses to arrive at a net income of 33 percent. If these numbers are comparable to your competitors, then you could conclude that you had a pretty good budget number. Remember that your competitors will also be budgeting and comparing their budgets to others in the industry. By reviewing specific period expenses, such as R&D, you would determine that spending 5 percent on sales and 6 percent on marketing was comparable to your competitors. You should be prepared to explain why you ended up spending up to 7 percent of net sales for the year in review.

Managers should be responsible not only for budgeting properly but also providing reasonable explanations as to the differences between budgeted and actual results. Example 10-1 shows mixed results. When comparing actual to budgeted sales, we see that sales goals were surpassed by 30 percent. While this favorable budget variance seems like good news, management must be able to provide a reasonable explanation as to why it happened. Was the sales budget "lowballed"? Did a competitor fail to provide a product? Did the market grow more than planned? Is this a trend that will continue? Are there any errors in the sales numbers? Does this increase make sense in light of the operating environment and your knowledge of the business?

Next, we should look at the operating expenses, which seem to have gone up significantly, resulting in a net income percentage of 32 percent or a 1 percent unfavorable variance. This miss is not good; often, Wall Street analysts will consider a miss in the bottom line more significant than a beat in the top line. Again, this performance measure is usually discussed at higher levels in the organization, but it will end up being your responsibility to come up with the reason for the bottom-line miss.

Horizontal analysis looks at the absolute and percentage change in the amount of each line item over one or more accounting periods. Example 10-1 compares the actual versus budgeted amounts. We normally concentrate on items where the difference is the greatest, either up or down. In Example 10-1, we see that net sales went up by $600,000, or 30 percent. The obvious answer is that we sold more product, and as we continue going down the statement, we see that cost of sales went up by $150,000, which seems reasonable. After further inspection, you will note that the cost of sales percentage went from 40 percent to 37 percent; while this is good, we still need to understand why. What did we do right? Did we miss booking some expenses? Was it the effect of selling lower-cost inventory? Were our planned cost reduction efforts more successful than expected?

Moving into the operating expense review, all categories—from selling to administrative expenses—are over budget by large amounts. The biggest overspend seems to be R&D. What happened there? Did we decide to spend on a project that was not budgeted? Were there changes in priorities or major projects? In this example, we see that even though it looks like we went on a spending spree, we managed to sell more and earn more as well. Not such bad news; however, for the purpose of this learning experience, we would have to question why our budget and review process failed to anticipate these possibilities.

Therefore, the first suggestion is that budget reviews need to be carried out at least quarterly. Large corporations have their entities review performance on a monthly basis. If the analysis on the financials in Example 10-1 was done on a quarterly basis, we might have noticed the increases in sales as well as the increases in spending. That quarterly analysis would have resulted in our questioning the current projects and may have even promoted changes in mid-year plans.

Vertical and horizontal analysis can also be done at a more detailed level. Example 10-2 shows a different, more detailed breakdown of the components of period expenses only.

EXAMPLE 10-2
SAMPLE DETAILED COMPONENT BREAKDOWN

XYZ Corporation
Operating Expense Variance Analysis

	Year 20XX Actuals	% Total Exp.	Year 20XX Budget	% Total Exp.	Variance Over (Under)	% Variance
Operating Expenses						
Wages and Salaries	$400,000	49	$300,000	56	$100,000	33
Payroll Taxes and Benefits	60,000	7	45,000	8	15,000	33
Rent and Utilities	35,000	4	24,000	4	11,000	46
Depreciation	17,000	2	15,000	3	2,000	13
Training	7,500	1	1,500	0	6,000	4
Expensed Materials	45,000	5	25,000	5	20,000	80
Expensed Equipment	25,000	3	10,000	2	15,000	150
Contracted Services	165,000	20	75,000	14	90,000	120
Other Expenses	65,500	8	44,500	8	21,000	47
Total Operating Expenses	$820,000	100	$540,000	100	$280,000	52

As you can see, the total period expenses match the data from Example 10-1, but show different cost categories. Using this data, we can quickly note which items need further investigation. Horizontal analysis shows that wages and salaries went up 33 percent ($100,000/$300,000), but we know that sales only went up by 30 percent. If the business is labor intensive, then you would expect labor to increase with sales, but why did it go up by 33 percent and not 30 percent or less? Perhaps you were using less experienced workers or more expensive overtime pay, or maybe you were forced to add an additional shift. Understanding what caused the variance is the first step in determining if further action is required. Another item that went up significantly was expensed materials, going up 80 percent ($20,000/$25,000), with a 30 percent increase in sales. This increase can have many explanations, such as a change in sales mix, increased usage while training new employees, or a misclassification of items expensed. In doing horizontal analysis you usually choose the items that have a large dollar or percentage variance first, such as we did with wages and salaries and the expensed materials in this example.

You can also use vertical analysis with this data; for example, you budgeted 14 percent of your total expenses for contracted services, but you spent 20 percent. Was this additional contracted expense authorized or necessary? What does this level of expenditure say about your cost structure? How do you control these types of expenses when conditions in the business change? Which category needs more review—expensed materials that increased by 80 percent but remained 5 percent of your total expenses, or contracted services that increased by 120 percent but only increased by 6 percent of your total expenses? Knowing your cost structure and the effects of changes in your production or sales levels is key in completing your analysis. The level and depth of the work will depend on your management's expectations and review process.

Every manager accountable for a budget should be able to analyze and explain the reasons for the most significant budget variances during a monthly or quarterly review. In these reviews, budget variances are reviewed, often line item by line item, and cost overages or under spending are explained by the responsible manager. Remember, the quality of the budget will influence the amount of information required to be investigated. If you did a good job budgeting and documenting your assumptions, and if you are following your plans and reviewing them regularly, you should have a good handle on any

STEP 10

explanations required when results do not go as planned.

Once all the departmental budgets and actuals have been reviewed, the finance group usually prepares a summary of the financial performance for the period, including an explanation of the significant variances. As a manager, it is important that you review this report and ensure that the explanations provided by the finance team are consistent with your knowledge of the operations. If the finance team provides incomplete or poorly documented explanations, it will come back to haunt you month after month. You must raise a red flag immediately if you do not feel their explanations accurately capture what happened during the period. They should discuss their explanations with you prior to submitting their report to the next level of management.

Progress Toward Established Objectives

As part of the budgeting process, your team and management agreed on a set of objectives and the associated plans to reach them. In step 6 we showed how to define and develop objectives and initiatives, which must also be reviewed on an ongoing basis to manage progress, document actions taken, and highlight any changes required to enable the company to reach its goals. Once again, depending on the size of the company and the number of teams or projects being worked on, you may need more than one meeting to complete the progress review. Example 10-3 shows a sample budget review document that can be used to monitor your progress against the plan using a stoplight analysis.

A stoplight analysis is a method frequently used to visually show how well a company is progressing toward its goals (Figure 10-1). Items listed in green (G) under a status column would indicate that they are either on track or completed, yellow (Y) would indicate an item is in process or needs review, and a red item (R) is one that has not been started, has been missed, may not be completed on time, or is a showstopper. Your team should define the parameters to be used when assigning colors to a monthly review chart to make sure everyone is clear on the measurements.

Example 10-3

Sample Budget Review Document For Q3

Company Name: ABC Sales Co.
Department: Marketing
Manager: Budget Year: 20XX

Review Period			
Q1	Q2	Q3	Q4

Strategy 1: Increase sales by growing the Latin American market

Action Plan 1-1: Identify products that are suitable for the LA market — Responsible: Joe Smith, Metric: # of products, Status:

0	2	5	
R	Y	G	

Action Plan 1-2: Hire and train bilingual employees — Responsible: Juana Diaz, Metric: Employees hired, Status:

0	4	7	
R	Y	Y	

Action Plan 1-3: Fund and staff South American regional office in Panama — Responsible: Lee Chang, Metric: Office opened, Status:

Y	Y	R	

Figure 10-1

What Is a Stoplight Analysis?

A stoplight analysis is a commonly used method to report progress toward objectives and the status of your action plans.

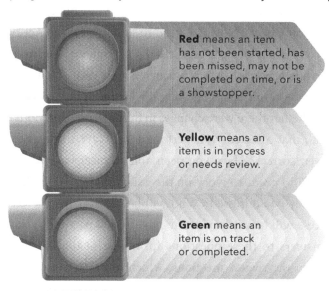

Red means an item has not been started, has been missed, may not be completed on time, or is a showstopper.

Yellow means an item is in process or needs review.

Green means an item is on track or completed.

STEP 10

You can use tables to show and document your discussion during the review meeting, such as those in Example 10-3. If all your projects show a green light, the meeting should go pretty quickly, because all your projects have been completed on time and on budget. In the first progress review of the year, your document will probably display a spatter of reds and yellows. During this period projects are usually in a startup phase or not scheduled at all for the period under review. As the budget period progresses, you should start reaching milestones and turning items green. The idea of a progress review is twofold:

- to see how projects are progressing and avoid any unpleasant surprises
- to discuss if changes or adjustments are needed to the plan.

These changes could be the result of changes in conditions affecting the company or issues found during the execution of the plans during the last period under review.

What Next? You Must Take Action!

The overall result of your review meeting should be a list of action or follow-up items. There is a business process commonly known as Plan, Do, Check, Act (PDCA), and so far we've essentially discussed the Plan portion of the budgeting cycle. The Do comes after the budget is approved and you start executing your plans. In this step, we focused on Check. Now, we need to understand the Act portion.

Once you have reviewed your actual performance in terms of financials and your progress toward achieving your goals, you need to act based on those results. During your review meeting you should have discussed whether there were changes in the environment, both internal or external, that affected your performance. Have those assumptions been proven correct? Have you been able to meet your objectives? If not, why? Who needs to work on the issues uncovered by the review? How will they be addressed? Who will be working on the issues, and what process will be used to inform the affected parties?

The answers to these questions form part of the documentation derived from the review meetings, which must be communicated to management. Depending on your organizational structure, changes to these plans may have to be formally approved by the next level of management, or they may just want to be informed and kept abreast of what is being done.

You must also inform the finance group. Ideally, your finance liaison should participate in any financial or progress review. After all, they are your business partners. However, if they did not participate, you must keep them in the loop. They are the ones responsible for determining and explaining the impact of missing goals, changes in expenditure levels, and updating the financial forecast. Whenever major changes to budgets are proposed, the finance team may have to submit new numbers and explain them to top management for final approval or as part of the quarterly or semiannual financial review process.

The Importance of the Financial Forecast

Part of your quarterly review will require what is called a *forecast*, which is a financial projection that usually incorporates the actual results year-to-date plus the expected performance for the remainder of the fiscal year. The financial forecast is used to determine if you will meet your budget commitments. It is prepared by examining the budget for the rest of the year and adjusting for any changes expected to occur as a result of your management review meeting. The forecast may or may not be used to measure management performance. Figure 10-2 shows the relationship between the budget and the forecast. Note the forecast usually does not extend beyond the current fiscal year.

Why is it important to incorporate changes to your operating environment in a forecast? The investor community carefully watches the financial information provided by a company as part of its quarterly reporting. Wall Street analysts use this information to make buy, sell, or hold recommendations, which may affect a company's stock price. If you provide good forecasts, and the company meets them, this outcome is generally considered good. However, if you underestimate or overestimate your financial performance, the market will probably penalize you, which may result in a drop of your stock price.

STEP 10

Investors hate surprises, whether positive or negative, because they send a subtle message that your management team is not in control. The market response to your plans is sometimes inconsistent with your financial performance. However, if you can provide substantially accurate numbers or have credible explanations for either misses or beats, the company is generally rewarded with more favorable responses from investors and analysts. Privately held companies also have owners, shareholders, and investors, and often use the financial forecast to understand how they stand in relation to the budget and the expected financial performance for the year.

FIGURE 10-2
THE RELATIONSHIP BETWEEN THE BUDGET AND THE FORECAST

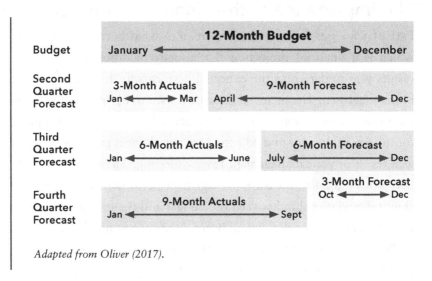

Adapted from Oliver (2017).

The forecast exercise is often carried out solely by the finance group operating in a vacuum. However, you, as a responsible manager, should work with your finance liaison to ensure that you agree with any changes that affect your area of responsibility and be involved in the calculation of the numbers.

Your Turn

The budgeting process does not really end when your budget is approved. It is part of a management control process that includes regular reviews to measure not only financial performance, but also track progress toward your company's objectives. This process should include a well-established procedure for analyzing the results against the plan and provide a mechanism to change direction if results are not being met or new opportunities arise. You should now understand the importance of identifying the causes of favorable and unfavorable budget variances and providing credible explanations to management. A clear understanding of your financial results signals to interested parties that management is in control of the business. Don't forget that after analyzing and explaining the variances, you must act to keep on track with your budget and meet your objectives for the year.

STEP **10**

Acknowledgments

We would like to thank Ryan Changcoco, senior manager, management development and talent development in industries topic, for his motivation to write this book. Ryan, without your encouragement, support, and patience during the hurricane aftermath, this book would have never been written. We would also like to thank Kathryn Stafford, developmental editor, ATD Press for her insightful review that improved the quality of our content and Melissa Jones, manager of ATD Press, for her copy editing.

Appendix
Glossary of Key Terms

Accountability: A condition where employees are expected to take ownership of their actions and be answerable for their decisions.

Action plans: Describe the specific actions that the organization will take to achieve their objectives within the established timeframe.

Bill of materials (BOM): A listing of the components and quantities required to build a product.

Black swan event: High-impact events, which are unexpected and unpredictable.

Bottom line: A colloquial term for net income. See *net income.*

Budget: A financial document that quantifies, in monetary terms, the action plans of a company over a short period of time (typically a year).

Budget assumptions: Guidelines and management expectations that underlie the calculation of the budgeted amounts in a department or work area.

Budget variance: The difference between actual and budgeted amounts. Variances can be favorable or unfavorable.

Business plan: See *strategic plan.*

Capital appropriation request: A form used to formally initiate and receive approval for a capital investment project. As a general rule, this project should have been included in the capital budget.

Capital asset: An economic resource that provides benefits to the organization over one or more years. It is classified as a fixed asset on the balance sheet. These assets are depreciated over their estimated useful life.

Capital budget: A structured plan for authorizing capital expenditures for the next fiscal year. It includes of the list of approved capital investments and their related costs.

Capital costs: Expenditures that will be capitalized as a fixed asset on the balance sheet and charged to the income statement over their useful life.

Committed costs: Fixed costs that result from contractual obligations, such as maintenance contracts or purchase agreements.

Cost of sales: The cost of products sold.

Cost rollup: A process done by the finance team, which calculates the manufacturing cost per unit, either manually or through a systems application.

Depreciation: A systematic method of charging the cost of an asset over its estimated useful life to different accounting periods.

Depreciation expense: Amount of depreciation that will be charged as expense on the income statement.

Direct labor costs: Represent the cost of employees who manufacture the product.

Direct materials costs: The purchase cost of raw materials, subassemblies, and packaging components, plus any other costs necessary to get the items into inventory.

Discretionary costs: Costs that vary at the discretion of a manager.

EBIT: A commonly used acronym that means "earnings before interest and taxes."

Effectiveness: A term used to describe whether the money spent achieved the stated objectives.

Efficiency: A term to describe how money is being used. It is typically reported by major spending category.

Enterprise resource planning (ERP): An integrated information systems application that records and monitors core business processes.

Factory overhead: See *production overhead*.

Financial budget: Consists of the capital budget, the cash budget, and the budgeted financial statements.

Fixed costs: Costs that do not vary with changes in volume.

Forecast: A planning tool that projects the financial results of the organization for a particular time period. The forecast usually incorporates the actual results year-to-date plus the expected performance for the remainder of the fiscal year.

Goal: A long-term outcome that organizations strive for.

Gross margin: The amount left over after recovering the cost of sales. It is the difference between sales and cost of sales.

Gross margin percentage: An important performance measure that shows gross margin as a percentage of net sales.

Headcount plan: A budget schedule that details the labor resources needed to achieve the work plan for the upcoming year.

Horizontal analysis: A technique to analyze financial performance that calculates a selected figure (either in dollars or some other unit of measure) as a percent of the same figure for a selected base period. This type of analysis can be used to calculate growth rates from one period to another.

Key initiatives: Specific projects that will move the organization to achieve its short-term objectives.

Key performance indicators (KPIs) or measures: Quantifiable measures that an organization uses to evaluate and communicate performance.

Key processes: Those activities that add value to the customer or are critical to the day-to-day operations of your organization.

Manufacturing costs: The cost to produce a product for resale; generally consists of labor, materials, and overhead.

Manufacturing overhead: See *production overhead.*

Mission: An element of the strategic plan that provides a framework to establish the long-term direction of the organization and defines the core purpose of your organization.

Net income: The difference between revenue and expenses, which is reported on the income statement.

Nonrecurring expenses: Expenses that are incurred infrequently due to a special circumstance, such as a one-time event, a systems implementation, a product recall, or a government fine.

Objective: Represents something specific that the organization wants to accomplish in support of a goal. Objectives can be long term or short term.

Operating budget: A financial representation of the short-term plans of the organization across all functions. It consists of the income statement and all supporting budget schedules.

Operating expenses: All expenses that are not directly related to product sales. They usually include research and development, sales and marketing, and general and administrative expenses.

PESTLE analysis: A framework used to assess an organization's external environment. PESTLE stands for political, economic, social, technological, legal, and environment. It focuses on those external factors that are outside the control of your organization but will have some level of impact.

Plan, Do, Check, Act (PDCA): A business model used to carry out continuous improvement.

Planning: A process that involves the identification of the goals and objectives for a specific time horizon and the strategies and action plans to achieve them.

Primary activities: Those activities that relate directly to the mission of your department or work area.

Production overhead: Manufacturing costs other than direct labor or overhead materials.

Production plan: Details the quantities of each major product that will be manufactured during the year and is expressed in a tangible unit of measure.

Pro forma financial statements: Financial statements prepared based on plans and assumptions about the internal and external environment. These usually include a balance sheet, an income statement, and statement of cash flows.

Qualitative objectives: Objectives that are subjective in nature and hard to measure in quantitative terms.

Quantitative objectives: Objectives that can be measured and tracked and are generally understood in terms of numbers.

Recurring expenses: Expenses that are incurred on a regular basis and can be estimated based on historical data.

Resource allocation: A key function of the planning process and allows the organization to evaluate if they have the right resources in place to support the business.

Resources: A term that includes the materials, people, equipment, facilities, and funding required to run the business.

Responsibility: The ability and obligation to carry out a given task, which is assigned explicitly to a specific individual to ensure the work gets done.

Revenue or sales budget: The monetary value of the product and services that you will provide to your customer for the budget period.

Sandbagging: A commonly used term in the budgeting process whereby a manager overestimates the amount of spending required to allow flexibility when budget cuts are requested.

Secondary activities: Those activities that support the primary activity, such as data entry, training, and supervision.

Semivariable costs: Costs that have a fixed and variable component.

Stoplight analysis: A technique that uses a stoplight metaphor to show progress toward organizational goals. Green means an activity or task has been completed, yellow means it is in process, and red indicates that an item is behind schedule or a potential a showstopper.

Strategic analysis: A thorough assessment of the external and internal factors that may affect an organization.

Strategic gap: The difference between the present and the desired future state of the organization.

Strategic plan: A document that describes the current and future state of the organization and how to get there.

Strategies: Mid- to long-term plans defined for a specific period, usually two to five years.

SWOT analysis: A framework commonly used to assess an organization's operating environment. SWOT stands for strengths, weaknesses, opportunities, and threats.

Tactical plans: See *action plans*.

Values: The basic principles that an organization holds dear.

Variable costs: Costs that vary directly and proportionately with changes in sales or production volumes.

Vertical analysis: A technique to analyze financial performance that calculates a selected figure as a percent of a base amount, such as sales units, sales dollars, or total assets.

Vision: A description of a desired future state that defines the long-range direction and goals of the organization.

References

Amazon. nd. "Career Site FAQs." www.amazon.jobs/en/working/working-amazon.

Apollo, B. 2011. "5 Timeless Principles: Revisiting the HP Way." Inflexion Point, September 30. www.inflexion-point.com/Blog/bid/74097/5-Timeless-Principles -Revisiting-the-HP-Way.

ASQ (American Society for Quality). 2018. "Plan-Do-Check-Act (PDCA) Cycle." http:// asq.org/learn-about-quality/project-planning-tools/overview/pdca-cycle.html.

Chase, R.B., and N.J. Aquilano. 1989. *Production and Operations Management: A Life Cycle Approach.* Boston, MA: Richard D. Irwin.

Drucker, P.F. 2009. *The Essential Drucker: The Best of Sixty Years of Peter Drucker's Essential Writings on Management.* New York: Harper Business.

FME Team. 2013. "PESTLE Analysis." www.free-management-ebooks.com/dldebk -pdf/fme-pestle-analysis.pdf.

Forbes. 2016. "The Wells Fargo Fake Account Scandal: A Timeline." *Forbes,* September 8. www.forbes.com/pictures/ejhj45fjij/where-wells-went-wrong.

Horngren, C.T., and G. Foster. 1991. *Cost Accounting: A Managerial Emphasis,* 7th ed. Englewood Cliffs, NJ: Prentice-Hall.

Jacka, J.M., and P.J. Keller. 2009. *Business Process Mapping: Improving Customer Satisfaction.* Hoboken, NJ: John Wiley & Sons.

Kanawaty, G. 1992. *Introduction to Work Study.* Geneva: International Labour Organization.

Morgenson, G. 2017. "Wells Fargo Forced Unwanted Auto Insurance on Borrowers." *New York Times,* July 27.

Oliver, L. 2000. *The Cost Management Toolbox: A Manager's Guide to Controlling Costs and Boosting Profits.* New York: AMACOM.

Oliver, L. 2017. "Planning and Budgeting." A management training seminar with OBA LLC.

P&G. 2018. "Q3 2018 The Procter & Gamble Earnings Conference Call." Q3 2018 Earnings Presentation. April 19. www.pginvestor.com/Cache/1001 235544.PDF?O=PDF&T=&Y=&D=&FID=1001235544&iid=4004124.

Packard, D. 1995. *The HP Way: How Bill Hewlett and I Built Our Company.* New York: HarperCollins.

Porter, M. 2008. "The Five Competitive Forces That Shape Strategy." *Harvard Business Review*, January. https://hbr.org/2008/01/the-five-competitive-forces -that-shape-strategy.

Shen, L. 2017. "Wells Fargo Says Sales Scandal Could Hurt Growth Permanently." *Fortune*, April 13. http://fortune.com/2017/04/13/wells-fargo-report-earnings.

Starbucks Coffee Company. 2018. "Mission Statement." Starbucks Corporation. www.starbucks.com/about-us/company-information/mission-statement.

Taylor, B. 2011. "How Hewlett-Packard Lost the HP Way." *Harvard Business Review*, September 23. https://hbr.org/2011/09/how-hewlett-packard-lost-the-h.

About the Authors

Lianabel Oliver, MBA, CPA, CMA, is the founder and CEO of OBALearn, an online learning company that empowers professionals with financial concepts to make better business decisions. With more than 23 years of experience in management training and consulting, she is a recognized expert in the fields of strategic planning, budgeting, cost management, and accounting. Over the years, she has designed and facilitated financial training programs for many Fortune 500 companies and professional associations. Lianabel has participated as a speaker in many national and international conferences. She is the author of *Designing Strategic Cost Systems: How to Unleash the Power of Cost Information* (2004) and *The Cost Management Toolbox* (2000). Her most recent publications include "Preparing and Defending Your Training Budget" (*TD at Work,* December 2017) and "Financial Skills That Every Manager Should Have" (*TD* magazine, June 2018). Lianabel holds an MBA from Stanford University and a BA from Yale University. She is a certified public accountant (CPA) in the Commonwealth of Puerto Rico and a certified management accountant (CMA) by the Institute of Management Accountants.

Eduardo Nin, CPA, MBA, is a seasoned financial expert and consultant with experience in high-volume manufacturing, process improvement, strategic planning, business start-ups, and personal finance. He has worked with organizations such as Hewlett Packard, Baxter Healthcare, and Coopers & Lybrand, among many others. He also facilitates courses on planning and budgeting for the nonprofit Asesores Financieros Comunitarios and speaks in many public forums on these topics. Eduardo has a BBA from the University of Miami and an MBA from the Wharton School of Business, University of Pennsylvania. He is a member of the Puerto Rico State Society of CPA.

Index

communication
  after the budget has been approved,
    99–106
  coordination between different parts of
    the organization, 10, 39–40
  establishing a safe environment, 47
  parking lot for keeping focused and on
    track, 57, 106
  team involvement in planning and
    budgeting, 10, 40, 47
competition, researching the, 51–52
confidentiality issues, 43, 83
cost of sales, 35
cost rollup, 35
cost structure
  departmental spending report review, 78
  nonrecurring expenses, 78–79
  recurring expenses, 78–79

D

data collection, automatic, 72
departmental spending budget
  analyzing department activities tool, 76
  calculating other expenses, 84–85
  cost structure, 78–79
  depreciation, 83–84
  estimating tool, 81–82
  labor costs, 82–83
  primary activities, 76
  report review, 78
  secondary activities, 76
  staffing requirements, 36, 77–78
  using benchmark data, 85
depreciation, 83–84
discretionary costs, 79
documenting budget-related activities
  assumptions, risks, and opportunities, 86
  cost estimation methods used, 86
  CPM (critical path method), 45
  importance of, 86
  line items that will be scrutinized, 87
  PERT (program evaluation and review
    technique), 45
  preparing the minutes of budget meet-
    ings, 105–106
  to reflect last-minute changes, 95
  team meeting after budget approval, 104
Drucker, Peter, 19

E

economic factors affecting business, 53
employees, pushback from, 102
enterprise resource planning (ERP) system, 33
estimating expenses, methods of, 84–85
expenses, recurring and nonrecurring, 78–79
external users of financial information,
    11–12, 117–118

F

facilities issues, 55
factory overhead, 34–35
finance group
  discussing performance progress with the,
    114, 117
  financial forecast, 118
  verifying planning figures with analysts, 90
financial condition of the organization, 56
financial statements, proforma, 11–12,
    28, 109
five forces analysis, 51–52
fixed costs, 79
forecast, financial, 117–118
Foster, George, 13

G

goals, 18–19, 72–73
government policy and regulations, 53–54
gross margin percentage, 110

H

headcount plan
  distribution of labor resources, 77–78
  as part of the operating budget, 36
Hewlett Packard Company, 18
hiring, 102
horizontal analysis, 111–113
Horngren, Charles, 13
"The HP Way," 18
Hurricane María, v

I

income statement, 11–12, 28, 109–112
information required for the budgeting
    process, 41–42
information systems, 55–56
interdependencies, 24, 53

production plan, 32
proforma financial statements, 11–12, 28, 109
progress, measuring
  key performance measures (key performance indicators), 72–73
  review process, 73
  sample budget document, 114–116
  stoplight analysis, 114–116
pushback
  from employees, 102
  from management, 91

R

RACI Matrix, 22
recruitment, 102
recurring expenses, 78–79
research, conducting, 51–52
resource allocation, 9, 71
revenue or sales
  data, 30–31
review of actual spending *vs.* budgeted
    spending
  focus on the "top line" and "bottom
      line," 110–111
  forecast, 117–118
  gross margin percentage, 110
  horizontal analysis, 111–113
  Plan, Do, Check, Act (PDCA), 116
  quarterly analysis, 112
  sample budget document, 114–116
  sample detailed component breakdown,
      112–113
  sample income statement, 109–112
  stoplight analysis, 114–116
  vertical analysis, 110–113
review process for the operating budget
  additional reviews and revisions, 92
  developing a plan B, 92–94
  frequency, 73
  limiting the amount of information
      provided, 95
  managing the, 94–95
  meeting with your manager, 90–91
  sample budget summary, 96–97
  team agreement regarding budget cuts, 91–92
  understanding the, 89–91
  verifying the figures with financial
      analysts, 90
roles and responsibilities

accountability, 22
RACI Matrix, 22
of team members, 45–46
rules for meetings, 43–44

S

sales
  cost of sales, 35
  data, 30–31
sandbagging, 8
semivariable costs, 79
short-term objectives
  key initiatives, 66
  qualitative objectives, 68
  quantitative objectives, 68
  time frame for, 65–66
  vs. long-term objectives, 19–20, 70
simplicity, importance of, 94–95
simulations, 11
SMART (specific, measurable, attainable, realistic, time-bound) objectives, 19, 67, 69
societal trends, 54
spending
  actual *vs.* budgeted, 108–109
  focus on the "top line" and "bottom
      line," 110–111
  horizontal analysis, 111–113
  sample detailed component breakdown,
      112–113
  sample income statement, 109–112
  vertical analysis, 110–113
staffing requirements, 77–78
statement of cash flows, 28
State of the Industry (ATD report), 85
stoplight analysis, 114–116
strategic analysis
  benefits of, 57–58
  business processes, 55
  economic factors, 53
  external environment, 50–54, 60–61
  facilities, 55
  factors to consider, 50
  financial condition, 56
  five forces analysis, 51–52
  government policy and regulations, 53–54
  information systems, 55–56
  internal environment, 54–56, 61–63
  key questions to ask when analyzing the
      environment, 60–63